HOME IDEAS

Kitchens, Walls & Windows, Bathrooms, Closets & Storage

ALEXANDRA EAMES & CAROL SPIER

Illustrated Books

A FRIEDMAN GROUP BOOK

BDD Illustrated Books
An imprint of BDD Promotional Book Company, Inc.
1540 Broadway
New York, N.Y. 10036

ISBN 0-7924-5845-1

HOME IDEAS
Kitchens, Walls and Windows, Bathrooms, Closets and Storage
was prepared and produced by
Michael Friedman Publishing Group, Inc.
15 West 26th Street
New York, New York 10010

Editor: Dana Rosen
Art Director: Jeff Batzli
Designer: Judy Morgan
Photography Researcher: Grace How

Typeset by Classic Type, Inc.
Color separations by United South Sea Graphic Art Co., Ltd.
Printed in Hong Kong and bound in China by Leefung-Asco Printers Ltd.

CONTENTS

PREFACE

Home is a personal place, a retreat and sanctuary from the outside world. It is also a practical place where the mechanics of everyday life are undertaken. Home should be a pleasant place, and it should reflect the tastes, interests, and personalities of the people who inhabit it while providing them with a comfortable environment in which to pursue their daily activities. The design and decoration of our homes is something that all of us undertake from time to time, some with pleasure and some with trepidation, because setting up a successful home takes both art and skill.

There are people who seem born with the ability to imbue their homes with beauty and character, who naturally assemble colors, textures, furnishings, and accessories that are pleasing and unique and then arrange them with effortless efficiency. There are others who look at empty rooms with panic, who know what they like when they see it but lack the ability or confidence to articulate it. And there are still others who have no trouble with the finishing touches but become confused and impatient with the underpinnings, having no idea how a home works or how the various pieces must fit together in order to provide for the inhabitants' needs.

Whether you are confident or tentative in your approach to the design of your home environment, inspiration and information are key players in successful decor. Even if you are blessed with unerring good taste, your eye should always be alert to interesting ideas; if you feel overwhelmed by the prospect of a new home or the remodeling or redecorating of one you already live in, you will need good advice as well. The four parts of *Home Ideas*— *Kitchens, Bathrooms, Walls and Windows,* and *Closets and Storage*—provide those who are ready for a new look with easy access to great ideas and useful information. Inspiration is presented in photographs and commentary on up-to-date approaches to home design, supplemented with enough basic technical information to enable anyone to plan and shop intelligently.

Home Ideas is neither a do-it-yourself manual nor a pretty but inaccessible style book; it is a book of decorating ideas and options that offers homeowners aesthetic and practical support for setting up their living environments. The principles of design are discussed, the difference between style and function is defined, and the practical mechanical requirements that underlie successful design are made clear. You—the reader—are encouraged to analyze your needs and situations and to define your tastes in order to create the mood and style in which you want to live. And you will see that good design is not only aesthetically pleasing but also functional, and that form and function are to some degree interdependent. No matter how extensive your decorating project, *Home Ideas* will help you to understand the nature of your undertaking; provide you with all sorts of ideas, options, and solutions to all types of potential problems; and enable you to approach the endeavor—on your own or with the help of a professional—with plenty of confidence and enthusiasm.

9

part one

KITCHENS

STYLE AND MOOD

The design of an ideal kitchen is a very personal thing, depending on the needs and desires of the cook or cooks and on various other ingredients as well. A person who is most concerned about creating a cheerful, attractive setting for family meals and gatherings will find that colors, patterns, and the design of the cabinets will be of the highest importance. Another person may wish for the greatest efficiency and a streamlined design for easy meal preparation and quick cleanup; to meet these needs, a contemporary space would be best, with cabinet doors that can easily contain things out of sight. The gourmet cook will look for professional appliances, ranges with large burners, and several sinks, all in a kitchen large enough for lots of activity. This room will be handsome, but the main attraction will be the beauty and flavor of the food produced in it. All of us dream of the ideal work space and are likely to include a little bit of each of the above qualities in our own kitchen plans. If you create your design carefully, you will have the perfect combination for your custom kitchen.

The overall concept for your kitchen will come from a variety of sources: books, magazines, show houses, the homes of friends, and the deep recesses of your memory. For example, all the kitchens from your childhood will surely influence your thinking and planning. Cookbooks or even vacations in exotic places will add images to your store of ideas: copper pans from France, painted cabinets from Sweden, or a stone floor from an English country house. Keep yourself open to many different ideas; gourmet cooks who delight in professional appliances can also dream of a setting for elegant entertaining.

To gather all of your thoughts into a cohesive and successful design, you should start with a clipping file. Whenever you see a magazine article about kitchens, circle the points of interest and file it, and include any references giving sources for materials so you won't have to hunt for them later. If you wake up at night with a brilliant idea, jot it down or sketch it. Throw samples into your file and order catalogs from manufacturers. If you can manage it without embarrassment, take pictures of the kitchens of friends or acquaintances whenever you see solutions that you think might work in your kitchen. A picture can prompt new ideas and make communication with dealers and contractors much easier.

You should allow time for all these elements to percolate in your mind and review the file from time to time, editing it and

Phillip H. Ennis

Most renovations of old houses include kitchen updates. Modern appliances and a contemporary layout can be combined with traditional cabinet styles, paint colors, and lighting fixtures that function well and also relate to the rest of the house. Although many old houses have had shining new plastic kitchens added, often in a new wing at the rear, these kitchens appear dated far more quickly than those that blend in and mellow along with the house over the years. On the other hand, don't feel you must go back to prior centuries just to get it right. One person will feel right at home with an ancient granite sink or the "Cadillac of Ranges" from the early 1950s, while someone else will much prefer the simplicity and easy care of plain white enamel. The wide range of colors and textures of synthetic materials available today allows for modern function within any style and can successfully simulate expensive, traditional materials such as marble, slate, and other stones.

The Spanish- and French-style kitchen **on this page** is quite grand, with high ceilings and bold architecture conveying a strong, coherent style generally known as Mediterranean. From the Aga cooker in its own alcove and the built-in wine cooler, we can guess that this family entertains large groups in a formal dining room to the left. The gleaming oak woodwork and traditional paneled cabinets set the style. Ceramic tile, often used on the walls and floors of houses in milder climates, continues the theme with a variety of large-scale patterns in vibrant colors and also adds to the mood. The dark green marble countertop is rich and slick, but at the same time the French country chairs pulled up to it add a casual element. Finishing touches include the pot rack, with its collection of copper, and the assortment of baskets, fruit stands, and containers on the counter.

reorganizing it into manageable subdivisions such as cabinets, appliances, flooring, paint colors, and even mood. This last category will include all those wonderful pictures of rooms that simply express a feeling you want to capture, whether sunny and bright or soft and mellow.

STYLE

The style of a kitchen will be dictated in part by the rest of the house. A Spanish Colonial home would likely have a kitchen with textured plaster walls and terra-cotta tile floors, like the Mediterranean-style room shown **above**, while the architecture of a modern house would be reflected in the style of the cabinets, counter material, and high-tech lighting, as in the slick black lacquer kitchen shown on page 18 or the sun-filled all-white kitchen shown on page 20.

MOOD

Mood in a kitchen is derived from many elements: the shape of the space, whether the ceilings are high or low, how dark or light the walls and cabinets are, and whether the surface of materials is matte or slick. If you are home only at night, you might prefer a cozy retreat, like the classic country kitchen on the right of page 17. If weekend mornings are special, sunny walls of pale yellow, like those in the city apartment on page 16, will make a rainy day brighter, while the serene, hearth-focused room in the early-nineteenth-century kitchen on the left of page 17 encourages lingering over the morning paper.

The choice of lighting can greatly alter your feelings about a room. Bright overall light may be desirable for cooking, while soft or dimmer light is more appropriate for dining. Once you have decided on the style of your new kitchen you can concentrate on its mood. Details can establish mood: plants in a window, a fire in the fireplace or Franklin stove, or flowers on the table. Notice the different details that establish the cozy and serene moods of the country kitchens mentioned above. And keep notes on mood details in your file so you won't forget to include them in your kitchen plan.

TRADITIONAL DESIGN

Traditionally designed homes are usually inspired by particular historic periods. Even a house built during the twentieth century is likely a revival of an early style. These styles originated in a particular country but have been exported around the world and altered by their contact with other design influences. In the sixteenth and seventeenth centuries, the powers of Europe launched their tastes across the seas to the new settlements in the Americas; later, these influences were felt as far away as India, the Far East, and Australia. At the same time, Middle and Far Eastern styles were brought back to Europe, creating a circular route of design influence. Today, Spanish style is evident in the Philippines; Japanese and Chinese style can be seen on the western coast of North America; and English style is evident in Australia. In the last few decades, the influences of Asian, European, Scandinavian, and African design have become even more widespread around the world.

The soaring height of the ceiling in this grand space **below** makes a traditional country setting seem more like a ballroom. The style is English, resembling a manor house, with the stained pine cabinets topped by a carved wood cornice, a fitting detail. In a room this large the cabinets must be bold and the island massive enough to hold its own. Bright white walls with a large expanse of window keep this vast cavern cheerful by day.

© Bill Rothschild. Designer: Beverly Ellsley

Formal

Cooking, dining, and entertaining are formal if executed with some ceremony. This holds true in both traditional and contemporary homes. Personal habits and preferences will determine how formal you wish your kitchen to be. If you dine in your kitchen, setting a table with candles and a centerpiece and using your best crystal, porcelain, and linens on a daily basis, your needs will be best addressed by a dressy room.

There are several elements that you can use to achieve a formal setting. Gleaming surfaces, deep rich colors, and polished metals spell formality. Symmetry, the arrangement of architectural elements, furniture, and accessories in even rows, pairs, or balanced geometric patterns, adds formality. Certain furniture styles, such as sophisticated designs developed in urban centers, are considered formal. Carved and gilded court-style side chairs carefully placed around a mahogany table will be much more formal than ladder-back chairs pulled up casually to a

pine table. Artwork, paintings in gilded frames, or decorative details, such as collections of china, silver, and glass, will give the final polish to a room that can be elegant as well as practical.

A room in a city apartment, even when very small, tends to be more formal simply due to its urban setting. The U-shaped galley kitchen **at lower left** is dressed up with glass-fronted cabinets, which give the illusion of space with the practicality of closed, dust-free storage. Handsome china and glassware on these shelves play a decorative role. The overall style and the mood evoke a butler's pantry in a big English Victorian house, a feeling enhanced by the walls beneath the upper cabinets and backsplash and the checkerboard pattern on the floor. The arrangement of the squares on the diagonal is easier to lay and visually expands the area, making it look wider than a floor that is all of one color. Even though the cabinets are simple in design, the addition of dramatic black appliances and classical urns provides a formal touch and makes reference to the black squares of the floor.

Country

Traditional country styles are considered much more informal than city styles. The materials are plainer and often less expensive. Furniture designs are not as elaborate, carvings are simpler, and the woods used are not as exotic. Pine, poplar, oak, and fruitwoods are the woods most commonly used in country cabinetry. Painted finishes are typical in rural regions of many countries and can range from a tinted glaze to folk art. The most familiar cabinet styles of English derivation have raised paneling, constructed in oak or pine with bold cornices and brass hardware. European country kitchens differ in the detailing. Swedish cabinets are painted in bright, light colors to reflect the most daylight. German kitchens have more carved wood with heart- and flower-shaped cutouts, fanciful trim on cabinets, and open shelving. The French and Mediterranean styles are bolder, with dramatic use of dark woods and ceramic tile.

The kitchen in the early-nineteenth-century American house shown **below** is still focused on its original cooking area, the hearth and fireplace. The room has been updated with a modern counter and appliances but has not lost its feeling as the central and warmest spot in this home. Wall cabinets are limited to open shelves between the windows and a shallow plate rack on the wall and mantel; closed upper cabinets might have required the elimination of a window and would have made this room seem small and dark. The soft green paint color works to unite the new cabinetry with the original woodwork, while the furnishings are comfortable and easy to move around. In the early days the drop-leaf table would have been closed up when not in use and placed against a wall and the chairs regrouped closer to the fire.

© image/dennis krukowski, Designer: Brenda Speight

© image/dennis krukowski, Designer: David Webster & Assoc.

The rural kitchen **above** is chockablock full of stuff to make you feel at home. One look at this kitchen and you can feel its warmth, inviting you into this casual and relaxed spot where you will get plenty to eat. The stove is unusual: a cast-iron, wood-burning cookstove lit early in the day and kept going until all the cooking is done. (This may be a reason why families living in rural areas once had dinner at midday.) The walls, or what little you can see of them, are sheathed in rough-sawn wood. The cabinets, also rough, are stained dark and recede into the background. Here is another example of upper cabinets with glass doors or open shelves that do not impose themselves on the limited space. Since this cook has a wide repertoire, every nook and cranny is used to hang molds, utensils, pots, pans, and baskets.

17

CONTEMPORARY DESIGN

Contemporary fashion has its roots early in the twentieth century with the International style. Form followed function in austere rectilinear shapes, and materials were displayed in their natural finish. Walls were pared down or eliminated to allow maximum movement, and large openings sealed with seamless plate glass let in sunlight and opened onto large vistas of nature. Today the modern movement has evolved into several looks, utilizing a wide range of new synthetics, streamlined appliances, and the latest technology in electronics and lighting. These are the kitchens where entertainment centers resemble recording studios, convection ovens and microwaves are built in along with trash compactors and water and ice dispensers, and refrigerators incorporate several climates behind foggy glass doors.

From modern construction techniques came Euro-style, which introduced frameless cabinetry, slick, glossy surfaces, and shapes related to automotive styling. In addition, a growing interest in gourmet cooking led to the professional look. In the early 1970s people began buying professional stoves, mostly black enamel and stainless steel, and in time, most domestic appliances were available in black. Today we have come full circle and the most popular appliance styles come in all-white.

Another contemporary trend is to borrow the best from the past—for instance a heavy-duty gas range from the 1940s or a collection of Grandmother's utensils—and combine them with the latest appliances in what is now called the retro look. Handcrafts are another contemporary mode, incorporating handmade cabinetry, pottery, glass, wrought iron, and woven linens in natural materials that express the style of each craftsperson.

Formal

As with traditional design, contemporary style can be rendered in a formal manner. In upscale city spaces or large weekend houses where evening entertaining is frequently on a grand scale, contemporary kitchens will be clad in glossy granite or marble, with polished brass hardware and shining chrome fixtures. The mood is stylized, with lots of glitter and shine and elegant glassware, china, and table linens. Even the cookware in highly polished stainless steel contributes to the clean, organized look. Small appliances are consigned to special cabinets and general foodstuffs are stored out of sight. An exception might be a fanciful espresso machine, a gleaming sculpture of chrome and brilliant color, displayed at its own work center.

© Jennifer Lévy

© Phillip H. Ennis

In the city loft kitchen **at left**, shining black lacquer cabinets contain and disguise the all-black appliances. Wall ovens, refrigerator, cook top, and sink seem almost to disappear when viewed from the living area. The appliances are arranged in a spacious U-shaped plan and are further hidden by the raised serving counter. Even the stools seem invisible when pulled up under the counter. The white pickled wood floor and pale gray granite countertops relieve the blackness by reflecting overhead light and expanding the feeling of open space.

While the kitchen **above** features a similar open plan, it offers a great contrast. The ceilings, walls, cabinets, and appliances are all-white. The gray marble counters and backsplash provide a strong horizontal band that brings the eye down to earth and softens the abundant daylight. Again, the cabinets and appliances blend together and all cooking paraphernalia is stored out of sight. The wall that divides the kitchen from the living area provides more storage and built-in niches for glass shelves and the television.

19

© Eric Roth

Country

Contemporary style relaxes in the country, with humbler materials and a more casual attitude. Not limited to actual country homes, this informal style can be adapted to city living as well. Painted cabinets and matte-surfaced plastic laminates in bright or light colors reflect daylight and sunshine. Bright enameled pots and pans are stored in full view. Dinnerware ranges from the simplest plain white to multicolored ceramics in contemporary geometric patterns. The flatware is straightforward, carefree stainless, and linens are textured wovens that go from washer/dryer to table without ironing. Bowls of fruits and vegetables and vases of flowers become works of art in themselves.

The all-white kitchen **at left** takes on a country feeling with hanging plants and a view of the garden. Filtered sun from the skylights washes light over all the surfaces and enhances the outdoor feeling. A casual sense of style allows for the usual toaster oven, toaster, creamer, and sugar bowl to remain on the countertop along with the colorful ingredients for the next meal. Pale gray plastic laminate for the countertops and natural-finished oak flooring relieve the whiteness and relate to the natural colors outside.

Contemporary country style is taken to sophisticated heights in the renovated barn **below**. Simple white cabinets line the back wall, while the island is painted a dusty green, a subtle contrast that nevertheless becomes the only strong element of color. The hanging green glass lighting fixtures confirm the color choice and, because of their symmetry, formalize the arrangement. In this setting an Empire clock and a pair of architectural fragments can coexist with a whimsical arrangement of old tools, pitchforks, and strap hinges.

21

THE SPECIFICS

We have come a long way from the kitchen hearth, the big fireplace with a crane to hold the family stew, and the labor that was required to cook large meals every day. We have eliminated the need to chop wood, carry out the dishwater, or shovel ashes. But many of our accepted conveniences today are refinements of rural settlers' ingenuity. Very early in history they developed rotisseries that functioned with weights like an old clock, washing machines operated with foot treadles, and apple peelers and portable ovens for baking potatoes.

Today, the choice of appliances and the many jobs they can do has exploded. The first step in helping you to clarify the choices is to start a second clipping file. This one will include only appliances and plumbing fixtures: the specifications sheets from dealers, pictures from magazines, and catalogs and prices. Eventually this file will also contain all measurements and technical details for installation. Start with the major pieces, refrigerator, range, sink, and dishwasher, but also collect information about the smaller, minor units such as microwaves, toaster/convection ovens, food processors, and blenders. They will all take up space in your plan and should be considered and accounted for early in the kitchen project.

MAJOR APPLIANCES AND PLUMBING FIXTURES

Ranges

The domestic range or cookstove refers to a complete unit that contains one or more ovens below, a cooktop at counter height, and a warming shelf, oven, broiler, or venting unit above. The first ranges were freestanding and were fired with wood or coal. They were usually positioned in front of a chimney and connected to it by a stovepipe. Some modern cookstoves still need an exhaust vent, requiring space for some sort of flue to be included at the planning stage. Even with the advent of gas and later, electricity, the standard range still contains its ovens below, with the cooking elements at table height. Today's ranges, whether gas or electric, come with a variety of electronic options for regulating heat and cooking time as well as options in the type of oven: conventional, convection, and/or microwave.

Some of the most welcome improvements in ranges today are the self-cleaning and continuous-cleaning options for ovens. The self-cleaning oven is heated to a very high temperature, and spilled food and grease are burnt into ash that is easy to wipe away. Continuous-cleaning ovens contain a special coating on the interior that allows for easier oven cleaning without the use of harsh chemicals. Self-cleaning ovens are the easiest to maintain.

Hi-Low, Slide-In, and Drop-In Ranges

There are three basic types of ranges. Freestanding ranges with upper ovens are called hi-low. The slide-in range is designed as one unit, with oven and cooktop that slide along the floor into a space between separate base cabinets. The drop-in range drops down into an opening in the countertop and the front of the cabinet. The edge of the range overlaps the countertop on each side so that food cannot fall between the range and the cabinets.

All of these types of ranges can come with an optional backsplash, but they are usually installed with the countertop backsplash running behind them. With the drop-in range, the kick panel at the bottom of the cabinet is continuous. Some range cooktops are now available with exchangeable modular units: griddles, barbecue grills, woks, and oversize burners for canning or stockpots.

Professional Ranges

The latest innovation in freestanding ranges is the availability of professional-style ranges that have been modified and are considered safe for residential use. They are still large, with four to six burners, griddles, a venting hood, broiler, warming shelves above, and one or two ovens below. But be aware that stoves designed for restaurant use are not insulated and must be installed against a fireproof wall. They create continual heat with several pilot lights burning constantly instead of electronic igniters. Be sure to examine the interior size of the ovens and note that a broiler is sometimes sold separately. If you are interested in a professional range but have never used one, it is a good idea to try one out and see if you like it.

© Eric Roth

If you think that you want to install a professional range, consider how it will fit into your kitchen space visually as well as physically. A special niche has been created for the professional range **above**, which has one oven, six burners, and a broiler above. The cabinet to the left is short enough to accommodate a separate gas grill. Easy-to-wash ceramic tiles line the rear wall, and a large custom-built venting hood covers the entire niche and draws off the cooking smoke and vapor. Although the equipment is professional, the ambiance has remained domestic.

Antiques and Imports

Ranges from the 1940s and 1950s are now appreciated for their sleek styling and heavy-duty construction, and there are dealers who specialize in old-stove restoration using old parts or machined reproductions. Those in North America with fond memories of Grandmother's kitchen will be thrilled with an old Glenwood or the DeVille model made by O'Keefe and Merritt, called the "Cadillac of Ranges" and replete with chrome detailing.

Early cast-iron wood-burning stoves are still in use in some rural areas, especially in places beyond the reach of electricity.

Newer wood-burning cookstoves in traditional and contemporary designs come in beautiful enameled colors in a variety of sizes. In a cold climate, a wood-burning stove can provide heat as well as an extra cooktop and oven space during the winter.

In a special category is the British Aga cooker, developed by a Swedish physicist to provide his wife with a stove that would be fast, easy to use, and capable of handling a variety of cooking techniques. Gas- or coal-fired, the Aga is always on and ready for use; the heat is contained by insulated sides and burner covers. Available with two or four ovens in bright enamel colors, the Aga is considered the Rolls-Royce of stoves. There is an Aga in the kitchen on page 14, and a four-oven Aga cooker in dark British racing green in the kitchen on the left of page 37.

Built-In Cooktops
Separate built-in cooktops such as the four-burner unit **below**, with its center grill shown open, became popular with the advent of kitchen islands. This substantial unit is installed in a solid synthetic countertop and is surrounded by ceramic tile on the walls. Downdraft vents on either side of the grill pull grease-laden smoke down and away from neighboring burners.

© Jennifer Lévy

Cooktops provide flexibility in the kitchen plan, allowing ovens that are not used frequently to be placed further from the counter work space. Even more flexibility is offered by the choice of fuel; the cooktop can be gas-fired, while the separate oven can be electric, or vice versa, depending on your cooking habits. There is also the advantage of being able to work at the cooktop without having to stand in front of a hot oven. Ventilation systems are available as part of the cooktop itself or are sold separately but installed next to or behind the burners.

Cooktops come in a variety of configurations, with two, four, or six burners. You also have the option of installing two burner units in different areas of your countertop. Modular cooktops allow for interchangeable grills, deep-fat fryers, griddles, rotisseries, steamers, and different styles of burners. In addition, individual freestanding burners are also made that can be plugged in anywhere on the countertop, much like a single-burner hot plate.

In the kitchen **above**, equipped for all sorts of culinary masterpieces, a grill with a downdraft vent has been installed in its own separate island. The two-tiered levels provide space for ingredients and easy access to the grill itself.

space is saved by installing the microwave oven in the cabinet above the cooktop. A handsome combination of white, gray, and black tile forms the backsplash that runs along the entire counter, visually lengthening the room. A brass rod from a bar-fittings supplier is a clever solution to the problem of damp kitchen towels as they can be hung to dry.

In the handsome kitchen **at right**, the same brand of cooktop incorporates six gas burners. The aluminum strip along the rear edge of the cooktop is the hinged cover of a downdraft venting system. The cover opens to reveal the control switch and a metallic grill to catch grease. The powerful fan and motor are installed in the rear of the cabinet under the cooktop, and the fumes are vented by ductwork routed through the cabinet to an exterior vent. In homes with basements, the ductwork can go straight down through the floor and to an exterior vent at the basement level. On the dividing wall at the end of the counter, a lively composition of black-and-white tile is combined with brass rods for a pleasing visual display that also provides storage for large pots, lids, and utensils. Also note the cornice at the top with the brass rod used as a plate rail.

Wall Ovens

Wall ovens are designed to be built in and are available as single or double units. The double ovens consist of two standard thermal electric or gas ovens, a single oven with a broiler beneath, or an oven with a microwave oven above it. Microwave ovens also come as single built-in units. Ovens with convection fans can function in both the conventional and convection modes; in convection cooking, fans in the rear, top, and sides of the oven circulate the heated air, resulting in faster and more even cooking. Since steam builds up in the oven, roasted foods stay moist and juicy. Be prepared for added noise with a convection oven, however, as the fans are on during the cooking cycle.

Some electric ovens combine microwave with conventional features such as baking, roasting, and broiling. The microwave aspect cooks the food quickly while the bake or broil modes

Cooktop Elements and Burners

Gas burners, conventional electric-coil elements, solid-disk electric elements, and electric induction elements topped with tempered glass are all available today. The latter requires the use of iron or steel pans only, but is very easy to clean as spills cannot leak down into the burner unit. Standard pots can be used on glass-top units with conventional coils behind the glass. Burner choice is really dependent on personal preference; if you are unsure, it is a good idea to inquire among friends and try out different burners before making a final decision. The arrangement of burners varies: standard two-by-two, with the front row staggered to one side with one large and one small burner, or in a fan shape with the two rear burners closer together.

In the kitchen **above**, a separate cooktop with gas burners and an electric oven were installed in the conventional arrangement of cooktop over oven due to limited counter space. Some cooktops are shallow enough to allow for this arrangement, but you should check with the dealer to be sure. Further counter

The tile-topped island **below** features a four-burner cooktop that contains a griddle or grill under a stainless cover at the center. Double wall ovens are installed on the opposite side of the island, which offers adequate counter space when removing hot pans from either oven. A vital element to keep in mind when planning a kitchen is to allow room for the oven doors to open. Other points of interest in this kitchen are the built-in commercial refrigerator with glass doors at the left and the climate-controlled wine storage unit seen in the passage at the rear. The most awkward and bulky pots and pans are conveniently stored overhead on a pot rack.

Vented and Nonvented Hoods
In kitchens with serious cooks and frequent cooking on a large scale, a good ventilation system will keep the room cooler, remove cooking fumes

brown the food and make it look more appetizing. Most ovens have a variety of timers, automatic cooking sensors, meat thermometers, and automatic roasting and defrosting, slow-cooking, or food-warming abilities. Computerized controls refine the cooking options but considerable time is needed to study the owner's operating guides to learn how to use them properly. When making your choice, consider the interior size of the oven. You may find that you are better served by one large oven rather than two small ovens. Self- or continuous-cleaning features should also be investigated when you shop for a wall oven.

and aroma, and cut down on soil deposited on walls and ceilings. This is particularly important for culinary methods such as grilling, broiling, deep-fat frying, or stir-frying in a wok, because oil and grease become airborne. A hooded area over the stove will help contain food splatters, and a nonvented blower system within the hood will filter out particles and recycle the air to the room. The most efficient venting system is ducted to the exterior of the building through the walls or the roof. As mentioned before, vented fan units called downdraft systems are also available for countertop installation. The size and power of the fan is dictated by the length of the ductwork; you need enough power to push the air the full length of the system. Filters are important with either the nonvented or vented systems, but metal mesh grills and filters must be washable (some go in the dishwasher) or replaceable. If possible, listen to the blower before purchasing, as the larger fans can be quite loud.

Refrigerators and Freezers

Refrigerators, big, bulky, and absolutely necessary, are the most difficult appliances to place in the kitchen plan. To incorporate them in an efficient work pattern, refrigerators must be positioned close to the sink and stove with ample counter space available nearby. Because standard units are deeper than base cabinets, they are less intrusive if located at the end of a row of cabinets or in a separate, deeper alcove. The more luxurious models and commercial units are shallower and wider, so they can be installed flush with the front of standard cabinets. Since the ventilation is on the front of these units, they can be completely boxed in. Commercial refrigerator units with the same depth as standard base cabinets are also available for under-counter installation. Optional cabinet panels, called trim kits, to match or coordinate with the cabinets can be mounted on the doors of built-in units.

Freezers are available above or beneath the refrigerator area or to one side. Accessories include ice cream makers, ice makers, and dispensers that provide cubed and crushed ice

and ice water or other beverages through spigots on the door. Small upright refrigerators that run on bottled propane gas are available for vacation homes without electricity.

The commercial side-by-side freezer/refrigerator **above** is built in within easy reach of the oversize island and its ample counter space. The doors are fitted with wood panels provided by the cabinet manufacturer to match the rest of the kitchen. The island cooktop has a fan-shaped array of burners, which allows more space for oversize frying pans and large stockpots, and the bar sink is a convenient extra area for washing vegetables and arranging flowers as well as mixing drinks. For buffet dinners, the bar sink can be filled with crushed ice and act as a wine or beer cooler.

Sinks

Fortunately, most of us have a personal preference when it comes to choosing a sink. Many swear by stainless steel, while others like only white enameled cast iron. There are also new synthetic materials in many bright colors that, although not as durable as the original enamel, are, with care, very serviceable and attractive. Many people are returning to old-fashioned stone sinks of granite or soapstone. Antique cast-iron sinks, some relegated to the pasture or junkyard, are also being resurfaced and used again.

Sink bowls come in single, double, and even triple units. With a large central island, a second sink can be placed nearer the dining area and used to speed up dishwashing. Bar sinks with smaller bowls are usually installed with tall, gooseneck spouts for filling tall vases, bottles, or stockpots. You may even want to use this type of spout with the primary sink.

A self-rimming sink is one that is dropped into an opening in the countertop. **Below** is a stainless steel example, combined with a white enameled single-lever faucet and a separate utility compartment to the right for flatware. On the left is a dispenser for liquid dish or hand soap.

The countertop and sink bowls **above** are both made of a solid synthetic material and are bonded together into one seamless unit. The swinging single-lever faucet here can reach both bowls, but without a sculpted lip around the bowls, some care must be taken so that water does not flood the countertop. The right-hand bowl contains a garbage disposal unit, especially convenient for disposal of waste generated when washing and preparing vegetables and salad greens.

shaped handle with a porcelain button at the center marked with an H or a C. These antiques can be reground and revitalized with new washers, but in the future it may become increasingly difficult to find an old-fashioned plumber with the knowledge, time, or tools to fix them. Many old faucets sold in antique shops have had the chrome plating removed and the solid brass beneath polished to a shine. Unless this brass is sealed with a protective coating or repolished occasionally, it will tarnish and turn a brownish green. An alternative is a modern reproduction that combines classic design with up-to-date function, as in the wall-mounted sink faucet **below**, which comes complete with its own old-fashioned soap dish.

When choosing your faucets, be sure to try out the controls to be satisfied that they are comfortable and that there is enough space between the handle and the spout for your fingers. Faucets developed for hospital use are very popular for kitchens because they can be controlled with a flick of the elbow, particularly convenient when your hands are sticky. Combining the ordinary faucet and spray into one unit, the white contemporary

The double sink of enameled cast iron **above** is set into a white solid synthetic countertop. Because of the raised lip around the edge, a dish drainer would work better set into one of the bowls instead of on the countertop. The dishwasher is appropriately placed right next to the sink.

Faucets Once available only in chrome plate, faucet sets now come in brushed or polished chrome or brass, gold plate, or bright enameled colors with double or single controls. In the early days of plumbing each spout had its own control, a cross-

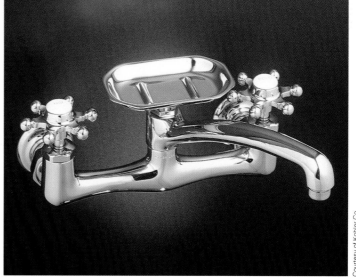

30

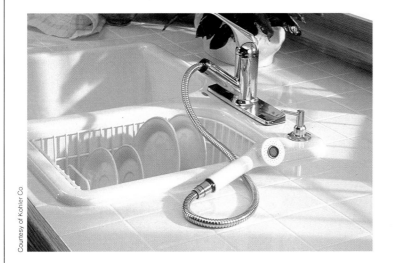

Courtesy of Kohler Co.

faucet **at upper left** is really a removable spray with a flexible hose. **At lower left**, a small bar sink is set into a tiny alcove. Dual levers on the tall spout are easy to use and do not take up much space.

When the older kitchen **below** was given a face-lift, the old enameled cast-iron sink was retained and the original faucet was reinstalled through holes drilled in the backsplash, which, along with the old drainboard, had been replaced with solid synthetic counter material. Because this material can be easily shaped with an electric router, it can be cut to fit unusual situations. Drainage grooves were cut on a slant, a bit deeper at one edge, so water will drain back into the sink.

© Jennifer Levy

© image/dennis krukowski

Dishwashers

The dishwasher is now a necessity for working families. For those that entertain on a large scale, two dishwashers can even be installed side by side to provide increased capacity. Dishwashers are standard in size and are either built in under the counter or portable, moved next to the sink on their rollers for water supply and drain. For right-handed people the dishwasher usually is installed to the right of the sink. Whether to the right or the left, it should be within easy reach, as most dishes are rinsed before being loaded in the machine. Manufacturers provide optional trim kits for the doors of dishwashers, with standard kits containing a choice of black, white, or a wood-toned colored or textured panel.

Washer/Dryers

Traditionally thought of as a kitchen appliance, the washer/dryer set is now more often placed in the basement, a separate laundry closet or pantry, or in the new and larger modern bathroom. However, the latest configurations of washers, which allow for installation under the counter or stacked in a narrow alcove or closet, can work comfortably within the kitchen plan.

MINOR APPLIANCES

Disposers and trash compactors are helpful tools but should be considered carefully before they are installed. If your kitchen is in the planning stage, check local ordinances regarding recycling to find out which materials must be separated; bins designated for glass, plastic, metal cans, cardboard, and paper will simplify storage and the delivery of waste material to the dump, landfill, or recycling center. Be aware that some municipalities with sewer systems prohibit sink disposer units. In a suburban or rural area, vegetable scraps can easily be composted for reuse in the garden using a plastic bucket with a tight-fitting lid stored in the cabinet under the sink. Trash that is suitable for

disposal in a landfill can be reduced in bulk with a built-in trash compactor like the one located behind the island in the marvelously well-equipped kitchen on page 25.

When planning kitchen counters and shelf space, consider in advance all the countertop appliances you will have and where they will be stored. Food processors, blenders, mixers, coffee makers, and can openers are all used daily, and they are often stored on the countertop. When planning a new kitchen, you might want to provide a permanent home for them on a shallow shelf built in above the backsplash. This would necessitate installing the base cabinet further out from the rear wall to allow the extra 8 to 10 inches (20 to 25cm) of depth for the shelf. An alternative is to store appliances on special pop-up or sliding shelves in cabinets located below the counter.

Toasters, toaster ovens, and countertop microwave ovens also take up space. If counter space is at a premium, shop carefully; some models are designed to be mounted under the upper cabinets, and there is even a stainless steel toaster that can be built into the wall and opens like a drawer. The owners of the small kitchen **at left** installed the automatic coffee maker under the upper cabinet to free up space. They also made a conscious effort to coordinate the color of the small appliances and accessories; although not always practical, this does make a difference in the neatness and perception of space in a small area.

Sticking to black, gray, and white, with coordinating tiles, floor, and cabinets, helps the tiny kitchen seem more tidy.

If you specialize in a particular type of cooking, consider setting up a workstation for the necessary small appliances. This baking center **below**, which also functions as a divider between the kitchen and the dining room beyond, is an echo of the early Hoosier cabinet. The Hoosier was the first "built-in" work center, with flour bin and dispenser, a pull-out counter, and shelves. Today's version has a pop-up shelf for the mixer and a warming oven that pulls out like a drawer for rising dough.

© Eric Roth

CABINETRY

The style of the cabinetry is one of the greatest factors in setting the tone of a kitchen. Once you have established the overall look, whether it is contemporary or traditional, you can then focus on the details that contribute to the atmosphere and practicality of your work space. Contemporary cabinets have flat, sleek surfaces that are devoid of moldings or intricate hardware. In contrast, the style of traditional cabinets, derived from early construction techniques, incorporates raised panels, crown moldings, pilasters, and other detailing.

STYLES: EUROPEAN VERSUS AMERICAN CONSTRUCTION

There are two basic types of cabinet construction. The European style consists of a box with a full-overlay door that covers the entire face of the box and is flush with the edges. The hinges are mounted on the inside of the door and are completely hidden. These cabinets have a sleek, seamless, and contemporary look whether they are made from wood such as maple, cherry, or mahogany or from shiny plastic laminate.

The refinement of the European style is evident in the kitchen **on the left of page 36**, with its striking combination of pale wood with charcoal-gray marble. The hardware is minimal, with brushed stainless U-shaped pulls. Rather than facing the appliances with matching wood panels, this designer preferred the professional look and practicality of stainless steel for the sink, wall ovens, trash compactor, and warming drawer. The stark lines of the cabinets set the tone for a work area that is space-age sleek.

Modern construction, appliances, and layout can be combined with traditional colors and hardware for a successful design in an old or new home. In the serene kitchen **at far left**, the European-style cabinets have simple paneled doors that give them a Shaker feeling. Glass upper doors with slim mullions and chrome bin pulls continue that theme. In a clever way of dealing with a structural necessity, the steel beam spanning the room is painted barn red and used as a very sturdy pot rack.

The American-style cabinet is composed of a frame attached to the face of the box. The doors are then hinged to this frame with a butt hinge that shows at the edge of the door. This is the same way solid wood furniture is made and is appropriate for a

© Jennifer Lévy

MATERIALS AND FINISHES

To simplify the vast choice of materials for cabinet facades, group them into three categories: wood, plastic laminate, and painted finishes. Painted finishes cover a wide range. Simple country cabinets can be painted at home with a paintbrush or sprayed with an airless sprayer. Cabinet manufacturers can apply multiple coats of glossy lacquer or mirrorlike polyester. Painted cabinets such as those from a British manufacturer **at near right** set the mood for this elegant country kitchen. A myriad of nooks and crannies offers storage and display areas for plates, cups, and platters as well as the space to disguise the more modern appliances. There are plate racks, tray racks, a wine rack, and open shelves with turned balusters and fancy cutouts. Glass-paned doors along the left-hand wall have a shallow center section, and the whole unit looks like an old-fashioned breakfront or a china cabinet.

kitchen in a period or traditional design. An adaptation of the American style uses a concealed hinge that allows the door to completely cover the frame and approximates the look of Euro-style cabinets.

The traditional ambiance felt in the kitchen **at right** derives from the combination of American-style cabinetry in all the latest configurations with old-fashioned details and richly colored walls. Raised-panel doors and drawers refer to eighteenth-century styling, while the layout makes this a most modern kitchen. A short but deep cabinet over the built-in oven fills an awkward space and connects the oven area to the rest of the cabinetry. The tambour, or roll-up panel, to the right of the oven is called an appliance garage and hides the food processor, mixer, blender, and other small countertop machinery. The crown molding at the top of the cabinets and around the walls is another traditional device that creates a uniform look, tying the various elements of the kitchen together.

© Melabee Miller/Envision

The mood is quite different in the Italianate kitchen **at upper right**, where a pedimented cabinet gives the air of ancient Rome. Pickled wood cabinets are hand-painted with classical designs similar to those uncovered at Pompeii and Herculaneum in southern Italy. A striped Roman shade is an appropriate choice of window covering, as it lies flat when down and does not interfere with the use of the countertop.

Wood cabinets with clear finishes can be contemporary or traditional in style. Clear (without knots) and knotty pine was used for the cabinets in the older house **at lower right**. Pine- and birch-veneered plywood is stocked in most lumber yards and is commonly used for cabinetmaking. More exotic woods veneered to plywood can be specially ordered, as can a variety of solid hardwoods. In this room, Shaker styling is combined with a dark green paint color for the floor and trim. Adding the pine panel to the front of the dishwasher makes it much less obtrusive, and the turned wood cabinet knobs are a nice detail.

© Jennifer Lévy

Plastic laminates almost always proclaim a modern, carefree kitchen in a contemporary setting. Conventional laminates reveal a thin, dark line along the cut edge, while the newer solid-core laminates have the look of a solid material because the backing has been eliminated. Laminates can also be wrapped around curved surfaces; in the dramatic kitchen **above**, white plastic laminates are wrapped around columns and the uprights of the center island. The room has a truly high-tech look, with recessed lips instead of hardware on the drawers. With all the strong architectural elements, the soaring ceiling in this room, the steplike cutouts high on the walls, and the intricate traffic pattern, we can imagine this kitchen teeming with activity. The polished stone countertop and brushed steel dining table add to the excitement of texture and shine.

In addition to the materials and finishes mentioned above, cabinets can also be faced in stainless steel, but these are likely to be quite costly. A gleaming example of a stainless steel kitchen can be seen on page 52.

CABINET FACE-LIFTS

It is not always necessary to completely redo cabinetry in order to revive a tired-looking kitchen; sometimes a thoughtful approach to refinishing, combined with new window and wall treatments, can be as effective as a more expensive renovation. In the casual country kitchen **at upper left on page 39**, door panels were cut out and replaced with washable curtains shirred on rods. A new countertop of plastic laminate, a new backsplash, and wainscoting effect a big change without too much expense. The wainscoting is natural wood with vertical beads, which is available in narrow boards or simulated in large plywood sheets. The gradual layering of old wooden boxes, an open flight of shelves in front of the window, and the shallow shelf above it provide storage for an ever-growing collection of early cookware and utensils.

A few very simple touches have updated the 1950s kitchen **at lower left on page 39**. Cabinets from the 1950s take on a fresh demeanor with white paint, new chrome pulls, and a new countertop. The standard cabinet next to the sink has been altered to hold a new dishwasher. The panel to its right fills in blank space and allows space for the door to open. To stream-line the countertop, the individual windowsills have been replaced with a continuous sill combined with backsplash. Note the understated but coordinated window and wall treatments and the checkerboard floor that pulls the look together.

CABINET ALTERNATIVES
Doors With Glass Panes

Doors with glass panes display fine china and silver, much like an old butler's pantry, and still protect them from dust and fumes. **At upper right on page 39**, glass panes are combined with oak cabinetry in a small but functional pantry area. Here, glass canisters with screw-tight lids add storage for hard-to-keep grains, flours, and spices.

© image/dennis krukowski, Designer: Walker & Co., SC

The glass panes need not be limited to clear glass. Opaque glass might be preferred by those who simply want to hide the jumble of foodstuffs and still have the reflective quality of glass. Or try glass etched in patterns to act as kitchen camouflage. Designs may be etched on the glass by professional artisans, or you can use stencils and a do-it-yourself etching kit. Pattern books of Victorian stencils are a good source for nineteenth-century-style kitchens, while Arts and Crafts and Art Nouveau patterns are also readily available and suitable for kitchen cabinets inspired by the early decades of the twentieth century. Frosted glass or glass etched with small geometric patterns can update basic cabinets and give them a high-tech look. In addition, new cabinet doors can be fabricated to hold panels of antique stained glass or can be fitted with new custom designs of stained glass that relate to the overall scheme, as was done in the kitchen shown on page 41. In a small galley kitchen or butler's pantry, limited space can be visually expanded by replacing the glass panes with mirrors.

Handcrafts

The handcrafted designs of individual cabinetmakers and homeowners result in one-of-a-kind cabinetry that incorporates interesting combinations of materials in unusual ways. The creative woodworker, working on his own or a client's kitchen, can combine old architectural details such as molding, panels, or window sashes into a new set of cabinets. Cabinetmakers can also combine handmade pottery tiles, stained glass, and hand-wrought hardware, available at craft fairs and shops, into the kitchen design. Even factory-made cabinets can be given the handcrafted look with handmade tile countertops, unusual hardware, or custom-made doors and drawer fronts.

Pale and dark woods form a patchwork facade for the handmade doors and drawer fronts **at lower left**. The two tones of wood are laminated in even strips for the countertop. Because water reaching unsealed wood will penetrate it and stain it black, any wood used next to a sink must be sealed with several coats of waterproof varnish before the sink is installed, and care should be taken to seal the edges of the cutout as well as the top surface. In this kitchen the pottery tableware and backsplash tiles have hand-painted designs, furthering the handcrafted look, but are available commercially.

In the unique kitchen **at right**, all-white cabinets set the scene for stained glass doors with natural pine frames. A landscape of trees, fields, and sky with bluebirds spans the length of the marble countertop. Should this homeowner ever decide to move, these doors can easily be removed and incorporated in new cabinets elsewhere.

Freestanding Furniture

Antique armoires, pie safes, china cabinets, Welsh dressers, breakfronts, and jelly cupboards are all freestanding pieces of furniture that provide kitchen and dining room storage. In addition, converting an armoire or chifferobe from a clothes closet by fitting it with shelves can make a handsome visual addition to the kitchen. One advantage of such a freestanding case piece is that if you are planning to move in the future, it can move right along with you, whereas built-ins are usually considered part of the structure of a house or apartment and are sold with the property. A deep cabinet can be adapted to hold a television, VCR, CD player, and stereo equipment. Chests of drawers that were designed for bedroom use can also do double duty as storage pieces in the kitchen area, with tablecloths best stored flat in shallow drawers. In addition, bureaus that are counter high can also serve as buffets.

© Eric Roth

Keeping up with the advances in entertainment technology, modern furniture manufacturers have designed cabinets to hold all the latest audio/visual equipment. Many pieces, although intended for living or dining areas, function well in today's expanded family rooms/kitchens. Styles range from formal, traditional tall chests to country cupboards with whitewashed, pickled, or painted finishes. The interiors of all these cabinets are flexible, with adjustable shelves, slide-out swivels for televisions, and shallow shelf storage for audio and video tapes and discs.

Although computers are most commonly found in bedrooms or separate studies or home offices, computer cabinets are also included in many family room/kitchen designs today. A workstation for the computer and related home-office work can be incorporated into the sitting area of a large kitchen. This can be a built-in cabinet or a separate rolling computer stand that can be moved about as needed. The possible contaminants of smoke and grease are not healthy for computer equipment, so these systems and the accompanying floppy disks should be covered and stored away from the stove and oven areas.

© Eric Roth

FUNCTIONAL INTERIORS

The interiors of cabinets and drawers are now designed more efficiently to hold the utensils and ingredients of modern cooking. Drawers have dividers and trays for spice jars; doors can be fitted with wire racks for pot lids; and there are lazy-Susan units for hard-to-reach corner cabinets. Tall cabinets contain multiple layers of hinged doors with shallow shelves to hold stocks of canned and packaged goods, while an existing closet in a kitchen or nearby hall can be transformed with wire hooks and shelving into a storage pantry. Many of these storage-enhancing devices are standard options in commercial cabinets; others can be purchased from specialty shops or catalogs and custom-fitted by homeowners or a carpenter, if necessary.

In the bright white kitchen that is located at **far left**, the two long walls are devoted to windows and a pass-through to the dining area, making the use of the remaining wall and under-counter storage even more important. A fake drawer-and-door front slides open to reveal space for salad plates in the top compartment and bulky salad bowls in the lower one. In another view of the same kitchen **above**, a bottom drawer is just the right size to accommodate packages of cereal. Basically a galley in layout, this kitchen gives the impression that it is much more open because of the cathedral ceiling, the skylights, and the long row of windows overlooking the garden.

COUNTERTOPS

The material chosen for the countertop in your kitchen must be durable, easy to care for, and attractive. Since it is highly visible, the countertop should be carefully selected to coordinate or compliment the kitchen design and coloration. The same style and mood criteria discussed in the first chapter apply here as well; slick, shiny surfaces are for formal kitchens, both contemporary and traditional, while more down-to-earth, natural materials are appropriate for casual, country-style rooms. The various materials come in many colors, which will appear quite different when paired with cabinets of different colors.

The practical aspects of the countertop material also need to be considered. Some materials are almost care-free, coming clean with a wipe of a sponge. The texture of the surface will determine its care; the grout lines of a tiled countertop will catch dirt, while a very shiny surface will need to be buffed with a dry cloth to remove water spots after sponging. Be aware that none of the common kitchen countertop materials can be used for chopping or slicing without marring the surface, and for reasons of health, a separate washable chopping board is always recommended.

STONE

Marble and Travertine

Marble and travertine are hard, crystalline versions of limestone, quarried in huge blocks and then sliced into large slabs about an inch (2.5cm) thick. The surface of the slabs is then ground down and polished. This surface can be matte for use on floors, or highly polished for countertops. The edges can be straight, beveled, or rounded in what is called a bull-nose shape. The sink for a marble counter can be dropped into a cutout from the top; this requires a self-rimming sink, where the rim sits on top of the marble and makes a tight seal. A handsome alternative is to use an undermounting sink, which is attached underneath the counter. The edge of the cutout is shaped and polished and overlaps the sink basin. However, undermounted basins are more widely available for bathroom installations.

Because limestone is porous and alkaline, marble and travertine absorb stains and can be etched by acids such as vinegars and wines; these counters require frequent wiping and waxing to retain a high polish. There is also considerable cost, due pri-

© Jennifer Lévy

Travertine is a textured version of marble with tiny holes like air pockets that are filled in before the slabs are polished. It is usually available in shades of tan and gray with lighter flecks. Travertine is veined with several colors running through it, and the pattern can be highly figured. It is an elegant material that is equally at home in classical period design and in a severe contemporary setting.

Care If you are a fairly neat cook, willing to wipe it often and apply polishing wax periodically, marble is a great choice. If you wish your marble surface to remain polished, a sealer of wax or oil is necessary, especially in food-preparation areas. An alternative is to not worry about water spots and stains, allowing the surface to develop a well-used, "antique" look. The lighter marbles, white with gray and tan veining, seem to show water spotting less than the darker colors, but food stains, cranberry and beet juice, and oil or grease will show up more.

Granite and Slate

Granite and slate are other types of stone quarried from the ground, cut into slabs, and polished. Granite is very hard, durable, and stain-resistant. It can be scrubbed with soap and water and rinsed clean, requires no special care, and is impervious to hot pots and pans. Granite surfaces can have a matte or textured finish or be polished to a high shine. The material is very cool and in the textured finish is very pleasing to the touch.

Granite comes in many colors, ranging from black and shades of gray to a rusty red, and always contains flecks or small granules of different colors, some of which can even have a glittering, metallic shine. Gleaming black granite is the highlight of the elegant kitchen **at upper left**. The stainless sink and cooktop are set into cutouts in the surface, eliminating any cracks or crevices that would catch crumbs. Other thoughtful details in this kitchen are also worth noting: frosted glass on the cabinet doors, the louvres on the bottom half of the pantry/

marily to their great weight, involved in the quarrying, transportation, cutting, and installation of these materials. The cabinets beneath a counter of marble or travertine, as with any other type of stone, will have to be sturdy enough to support this weight. Sometimes the floor joists, the structures that support the kitchen floor, will have to be reinforced to support large areas of stone counters.

Marble comes in many colors, depending on the country and region of origin. There are whites, grays, and blacks, as well as a variety of rusts, ochers, greens, and browns. Every piece is slightly different and is patterned with veins and flecks in other colors. When selecting marble, try to see the actual piece before it is custom-cut for your job, for you may prefer the figuring of one piece over another. In addition to its beauty, one singular advantage of marble is that it makes a wonderful surface for rolling out pastry dough. Since it is so cool, the shortening in the dough does not get too soft and the dough retains its shape.

kitchen **below**, dark gray granite is used for counters and backsplash. A unique feature is the natural wood band that edges the countertops, matching the oak of the cabinets and floors and creating a look that is up-to-date but warm and relaxed.

Slate has many of the same qualities as granite, although it is not as hard and should be sealed before use as a kitchen counter. As it comes from the ground, slate is composed of many thin layers. Slate countertops are made the same way as early blackboards, by driving a small wedge into the edge of a slab of slate, splitting the layers apart and revealing a naturally smooth surface. Today this surface is attractive for countertops but is also easily scratched by metal or other hard utensils.

closet doors on the right, and the brass-and-fluted-glass lighting fixtures over the island. Light gray tile covers the backsplash and wall above the counter, bringing out the speckled tones in the granite.

The very different but equally sophisticated room **above** also features polished granite for the countertops, with the repetition of the rich rust color in the practical ceramic tile floor helping to expand the width of the room. The counter has a rounded or bull-nosed edge, a self-rimming stainless steel sink, and a slide-in range with microwave oven above. In the large contemporary

47

Slate tends to look less ostentatious or grand than the other stones. **Below**, the setting is contemporary but the feeling is definitely Shaker. Satin-finish cherry wood for the window trim and cabinets is set off by a simple black slate counter and back-splash. In this case, the slate is cut into small "tiles" and laid in a random fashion. The subtle curve from backsplash to windowsill is a particularly handsome detail. Black iron pulls are a fine finishing touch.

© Jennifer Levy

TILE

Ceramic tile is also a popular choice for countertops. Prices can range from inexpensive for standard 4-by-4-inch (10-by-10cm) tiles in solid colors designed primarily for bathroom walls and floors to quite expensive for handmade or hand-painted tiles. Many of the most elegant tile patterns come from Italy, a country also known for its ceramic tableware and pottery. If you are deal-ing with an individual potter, you can even have dinnerware, bowls, and teapots made to match the tiles for walls and coun-tertops. Styles of ceramic tiles are extremely diverse; they can be very elegant, perhaps with large scrolling patterns with a Mediterranean look, or naive, with folk art patterns of animals and flowers. In the fresh, sunny kitchen **at near right**, rose and white ceramic tiles are arranged in an alternating pattern of tiles with blank centers and tiles with flowers. The rounded edge band is made of hardwood pickled with a wash of white stain and varnished.

The spaces between tiles are filled with grout, which can be thick or thin depending on the tile design and the use of the area. For countertops, a very thin grout line is easier to keep clean. Grout can be textured or smooth and comes in a number of colors. Grout sealer that is brushed onto the grout lines and helps to resist stains is available, but light-color grouts almost always end up a bit darker where food is prepared.

Care A tile countertop usually needs only to be wiped clean with a sponge. If there is a buildup of soil in the grout lines, use a scrub brush and a nonscratch powder or liquid cleanser to get at the dirt, then wipe them clean with a damp sponge.

WOOD

With modern varnishes and thoughtful care, wood counters can be long-wearing. A wood countertop is made of solid wood boards or strips laminated together, and a hardwood with a

strips, butcher block style, maple is the choice for the working kitchen **below**. A collection of round and pig-shaped cutting boards are provided to prevent damage to the finished counter. Note the good use of detail that makes this kitchen work visually as well as practically. The commercial-style stove is a four-burner model with a small griddle under the chopping block on the left and a large oven below. Four rows of tiny ceramic tiles are set in a checkerboard pattern above plain white tile, making an extra tall backsplash. The cabinet doors echo the window and the floor complements the neutral counter.

closed grain is the most practical material. Wood is very sensitive to moisture in the air, expanding and contracting with the level of humidity, so there is always the chance of warping or of the seams opening up. In addition, water that is allowed to soak into wood will turn it black. Hardwoods such as maple will resist moisture better than softwoods like pine, which should be sealed with varnish. Several coats of waterproof varnish are necessary, with particular attention paid to the area surrounding the sink and the seam where the backsplash meets the counter at the back of the sink. A wood countertop should be finished before the sink is installed. If the wood is sealed and varnished, be sure to provide a separate cutting board so guests are not tempted to slice directly on the counter.

Maple has long been used for butcher blocks and is the most common wood used for countertops; it can be finished or left unfinished to take on stains, scratches, and slices. Laminated in

Other hardwoods, such as mahogany or cherry, can also be used, but they are somewhat more expensive. The hardwood countertop **at left** has a ceramic tile insert for hot pots and pans next to the stove, a device that could be used to protect any counter from burns. The stove itself is an old-fashioned champ with ovens galore and six burners. The brass pole above the backsplash is a simple and convenient pot rack.

Care Wood finished with modern varnish can simply be wiped clean with a damp sponge. Abrasive cleansers are to be avoided. If the varnish is worn, cut, or scratched, it may have to be sanded and refinished.

SYNTHETIC MATERIALS

Cultured Marble
This material has the look of marble but is a synthetic composition with a thin polished surface. If treated gently, it will provide service but will not be as long-wearing as plastic laminates or solid synthetic materials.

Solid Synthetic Material
Solid synthetic materials are known better by their brand names, such as Corian by Du Pont or Fountainhead by Nevamar. They are solid, composed of the same material all the way through without a separate backing or top surface. Therefore, they can be cut, sanded, and polished, and repaired or repolished if cut or burned. With the use of a fairly new tool, the electric router, these solid materials can be cut with straight, beveled, or shaped edges such as the bull nose (rounded) or ogee (an S-shaped contour often found on fine furniture). Grooves can be routed into the material and strips of contrasting color or material inlaid and glued in the grooves. A countertop can have an edge of contrasting color and pattern or even a metal strip in brass or chrome finish. Since this material can be glued or bonded to itself with almost invisible seams, large or oddly shaped counters are possible. Sinks molded from the same material can be undermounted and become an integral part of the countertop.

In the kitchen **below**, an understatement in white on white on white, a pristine combination of subtle textures is completed by a countertop of white solid synthetic. The polished brass bar sink is undermounted, and a false drawer on the front of the cabinet balances the design.

© Phillip H. Ennis

Care Clean solid synthetic material with a damp sponge. If stained, use a nonabrasive polishing cleanser. Sand out scratches or cuts with very fine wet/dry sandpaper or rosin paper and then polish with continuously finer grades of paper.

Plastic Laminates

About the least expensive and most practical of all countertop materials, plastic laminate (also known by the brand name Formica) is a thin sheet comprised of many layers of plastic material that have been bonded together with layers of paper under great pressure. To make a countertop, the laminate is glued to a plywood or particleboard substrate, and the edges are covered with a thin strip of matching or contrasting laminate. Most laminates have a brown backing material that shows as a thin dark line at the cut edge, with the top layer containing the color and pattern. More recently, solid-core laminates have been developed with the same color and pattern throughout the thickness and without the backing. With this change, the dark line has been eliminated, and surface wear is less noticeable.

For boldly shaped edge bands, solid-core laminates can be glued in several layers and sculpted with a router in a manner similar to the solid synthetic material mentioned earlier. Two or more colors can be combined to give countertops contrasting edge bands or inlaid on the top surface to form patterns. All laminates can have a rounded edge band that is continuous with the top of the counter. The color and design range for plastic laminates is almost endless, with granite and marble look-alikes particularly popular now. Plastic laminates come in glossy, matte, or lightly textured finishes, with the glossy surfaces showing wear more quickly than the matte finishes.

Care To clean a glossy laminate, use a damp sponge and then polish away water spots with a soft towel. Stains on the matte surface can be removed with a nonabrasive cleaner.

STAINLESS STEEL AND COPPER

Metal countertops can be custom-fabricated in stainless steel or copper. Stainless steel requires minimum care but can scratch easily, so it cannot be used as a cutting surface. Copper needs to be polished often and should be treated with the same care as copper pots or copper-bottomed pans. Early sinks and drain boards were made from solid wood and lined with copper sheeting hammered to fit. If they have not corroded too badly, these early countertops can still be used and will lend an air of authenticity to turn-of-the-century-style kitchens.

On the other hand, metal surfaces can give a kitchen an industrial or slick professional ambience, as in the one **at left**, where stainless steel countertops are combined with laminate-clad cabinets in a brushed stainless steel finish. The look is high-tech and very city-slick. Even the table on the right is made of space-age tempered striped glass.

PROFILES, MOLDING, AND TRIM

A number of the countertops in this chapter are trimmed with wood molding. While the edges of countertops are often an integral part of the top surface or comprised of the same material,

with tile, marble, wood, and plastic laminates, a contrasting band of wood molding can be an inexpensive as well as decorative edge finish. Stock moldings in a variety of shapes in clear pine can be found at the lumber yard, while more exotic woods can be ordered from specialty suppliers. This border can be varnished or painted.

WORK CENTERS

When deciding on the countertop material for work centers, the first thing to consider is how that area is going to be used. Some materials are better suited to certain tasks. For example, because of recent concern over salmonella contamination and possible food poisoning, wood chopping blocks are not recommended for cutting raw meat or poultry. A separate plastic board that can be washed with hot soapy water can be more easily disinfected and therefore makes a better choice. Wooden boards are fine, however, for slicing bread or cutting vegetables and fruits.

It is sometimes possible to give a particular area a special treatment; for rolling out pastry, polished marble has long been a favorite. If a whole counter of marble is too costly, consider a cutout in the countertop for a smaller marble insert. An area of countertop that is heat-resistant is helpful next to the range. With the advent of the dishwashing machine, drain boards have been eliminated from the edges of sink areas, but a sloping drainage area is ideal for large pots and pans. A drain board such as the one that was added to the old sink with the wall-mounted faucet on page 31 is also convenient for arranging flowers and spraying small house plants. A beverage center or bar need not take up much counter space, but the counter surface should be resistant to alcohol or coffee and tea stains. Often designed as a separate cabinet for an espresso machine or electric coffee-maker, this small area can be lined with patterned ceramic tile without breaking your budget.

FLOORING

Considering the traffic, food spills, and tracked-in sand, pet hair, and grass clippings that the typical kitchen floor must endure, it must be rugged and easy to clean. The floor should also be comfortable and good-looking. The final choice of a flooring material will be based upon all of these criteria, but the weight of each factor really depends, of course, on the type of house, the location, and the life-style of the family that lives there. A kitchen that opens onto a backyard or garden, or one near the beach or a child's sandbox, will be plagued by grit, with every footstep like a sheet of sandpaper rubbing the floor surface and grinding down the finish. (Needless to say, the best thing that ever happened to flooring was the invention of the vacuum cleaner. The more frequently a floor is vacuumed, the longer it will last.) Moisture is also destructive to a floor, inflicting the most damage in front of the sink, between the sink and dishwasher, or in the laundry area, so a waterproof coating is most important. The third menace to kitchen flooring is food, particularly those substances that leave permanent stains. Cranberry juice, beets, fat, salad oil, coffee, tea, and many more substances have the potential to leave large spots. Again, the best protection is a durable water- and stain-resistant finish coat that will repel stains before they sink in. A damp sponge used as soon as spills occur will help to eliminate damage to the floor as well.

VINYL AND RUBBER TILE

Vinyl and, less commonly, rubber tile have long been practical choices for residential and commercial floors. Standard 8- and 12-inch (20 and 30cm) square tiles in many colors and patterns can be combined endlessly in different compositions. In terms of practicality, the lighter colors will show shoe scuffs the most, and darker colors tend to reveal dust; the ideal is a medium tone with a small overall pattern to hide the dirt. Maintenance of vinyl tile floors is easiest with an electric polisher that can be used for both washing and buffing. A waxed finish offers the most protection, although most vinyl tile has a stain- and moisture-resistant surface. An advantage of using individual tiles is that a tile can be lifted up and replaced should it become damaged. Be aware that moving large appliances can scrape or tear a vinyl floor.

The most common basic tile layouts are two colors arranged in a checkerboard pattern or solid centers with contrasting bor-

© Daniel Eifert. Designer: Kate Altman

ders. Add more colors or mix a couple of patterns and the design possibilities become more and more intriguing. You can see a very simple checkerboard variation in the kitchen **above**, where black and white tiles have the added twist of royal blue. The bold pattern draws attention to the floor and seems to widen the space, and the room is unified by having the same colors repeated in the horizontal band of ceramic tile along the backsplash. Also worthy of note in this small kitchen is the slide-out tray to the left of the stove that provides additional counter space.

VINYL SHEET FLOORING

Vinyl sheet flooring is the latter-day version of coated floor cloths and linoleum. Since vinyl sheet goods are manufactured in widths of 6 and 12 feet (2 and 4m), they can often be installed without seams, which prevents moisture from seeping through to the backing, and so offers the best protection from spilled liq-

uids. Sheet goods can be installed with or without glue. Seams are always glued, and in areas of heavy traffic, the edges may be glued to prevent movement of the sheet.

Sheet flooring is also called resilient flooring since it is softer and less fatiguing to stand on than hard floors. Available in several thicknesses, the most expensive sheet flooring has a cushioned backing that also functions as insulation underfoot and is not icy cold to bare feet. One large advantage of vinyl sheet flooring is that the homeowners can install it without professional help by carefully following the instructions. The only tools required are a ruler and utility knife, and the job can easily be done in one day.

Vinyl sheet flooring is available in colors and patterns that imitate natural materials such as marble, stone, and brick as well as in fanciful designs based on traditional floral or old-fashioned stencil designs. The pattern used for the country floor **at near right** is simulated marble in three shades, combined in an elaborate checkerboard pattern. This flooring material has the advantage of a no-wax finish and requires only vacuuming and damp mopping to keep it shiny; a little nonscratch cleanser can be used for tougher stains.

WOOD

Long before the invention of tough, waterproof urethane, acrylic, and polymer floor finishes, wood kitchen floors were usually painted or covered with linoleum or washable rag rugs. In colonial times, wood floors throughout a house were left unfinished and cleaned by sprinkling sand on them and then sweeping up the sand. Sometimes the floors were washed and bleached, but often they were left to build up a natural patina. As paint became more readily available and less expensive, it became the finish of choice. It was practical, and the bright colors were welcome in city and country homes alike. The earliest wood floors were made with wide boards cut from first-growth trees. With the nineteenth-century invention of the circular saw,

from red mahogany to black walnut. A "pickled" floor has a white stain that is applied and then wiped off to reveal the grain of the wood. Urethane varnishes tend to yellow over time, and some floor finishers apply fewer coats over pickled floors to mini-mize this effect. The result is that a pickled floor may wear more quickly than conventionally stained and finished floors. But new interpenetrating polymer coatings are tougher than urethanes and will not yellow. They are more expensive than urethanes but are water-based and easier to apply, and they dry quickly.

In the kitchen **below**, the nail heads on the knotty pine floor of random-width boards have been left showing. Reproduction "rose head" nails are often chosen for their old-fashioned deco-rative appeal. Pine is a very soft wood and should be expected to scratch and wear in the heavily trafficked areas between sink, refrigerator, and stove. Varnishes offer some protection and make pine floors easier to clean but do not entirely eliminate the possibility of dents or scrapes.

wood could be cut into narrow strips that allowed for less warp-age and made it possible to cut out knots and flaws without much waste.

The most common woods for flooring are pine, installed in wide boards, and narrow-strip oak. Other woods such as cherry, fir, and maple—the latter most often used for dance floors and gymnasiums—are still available.

Natural Finish

The plastic coatings designed for modern wood floors come in satin and gloss finishes. The satin is not as shiny as the gloss and is especially appropriate on wide-board floors. Several coats of varnish must be laid down on a wood floor to build up a durable finish, and if a darker shade of wood is desired, it must be stained before the protective coating is applied. Stains range

© Bill Rothschild. Designer: Carolyn Guttila

Painted and Stenciled Finish

Deck and porch floor paint is an inexpensive way to add color and pattern to an existing wood floor and is durable enough to take the usual kitchen abuse. Traditional deck paints come in greens, barn reds, blues, tans, and grays in medium to high gloss. New acrylic epoxy paints that are designed for outdoor and indoor application are now available with a matte or satin finish. The higher the gloss, the easier the care, and for extra protection a satin or gloss clear varnish can be applied over the paint. Be sure the varnish chosen is compatible with the paint and be aware that the varnish layer may alter the color of the paint somewhat.

Any number of effects can be achieved when a floor is painted. A solid coat adds color and masks worn, ill-matched, or poor-quality flooring with a minimum of fuss. Simple tilelike patterns, such as the one in the old-fashioned kitchen in a seashore summer house **at near right**, are not difficult if time is taken to lay them out properly before the brush touches the paint. Here the room was updated with fresh white paint on walls, floor, and trim, and after laying out a grid to get the design straight, little black squares were stenciled in rows on the floor. For durability, the area under the huge gas stove is protected by gray ceramic tile. Another point of interest is the use of marble on both the counters and as a tabletop on an old iron table base.

In the small vacation house **on the left of page 59**, a wide-board pine floor gains a ruglike design of gray squares surrounded by a matching border. The steps taken to achieve this natural-plus-paint look involved sanding the floor, applying the gray paint, and then applying several coats of varnish.

Decorative borders and fields (the center of the design) can be added freehand or with stencils. Artists' acrylic paints may be used for the decorative designs but should be coated with protective varnish to hold up under traffic. **On the right of page 59**, the butler's pantry in an old house now serves as a breakfast room next to the kitchen. The floor is painted green

© Phillip H. Ennis

with a stenciled trellis border and bunches of daisies painted by hand. The wonder of butler's pantries is that they had storage of all sorts and sizes for china, silver, and glassware, and countertops where the tea and breakfast trays were set up. The built-in cabinet on the righthand side is the original icebox, once kept cool by a daily delivery by the ice man.

CERAMIC TILE

Ceramic floor tile is durable, practical, and very beautiful. Mass-produced tiles run the gamut of designs and colors and are not too expensive. Handmade tiles from Europe and Mexico cost

comes in several colors, and the width and color of the grout lines will affect the look of the overall floor. Some lighter grout colors may require a clear sealant. Tiles must be laid on a flat surface without bumps or holes, and a thin underlay of plywood is usually nailed or glued to the existing floor to provide a firm base. Tiles are often used in warm climates because they are so cool to the touch; by the same token, they can be very cold in winter and are also hard on the feet and legs.

more but can have great impact used in a small area, such as a border or a section in the center of the floor. Quarry tiles are terra-cotta tiles that are unglazed. They come in large squares and need to be sealed with a varnishlike coating before use. When selecting tiles, be sure they are designated for floor use; wall tiles may be thinner with a more fragile glaze and will not hold up under foot traffic. Even though tiles should last a lifetime, it is a good idea to keep them clean of grit or sand so the glaze does not wear away.

Many tiles consist of a porous ceramic base with a hard glaze coat on the surface. Other tiles are made of one material all the way through and are fired at a higher temperature. The surface of these tiles is matte, and although they are sometimes a bit more difficult to clean, they will never wear out. Grout material

that make the installation easier and faster. Glazed tiles, also 2 inches (5cm) in size, are used for the countertop, which is edged with a wooden band finished to match the cabinets.

STONE AND BRICK

Stone flooring includes granite, marble, travertine, and slate pavers, pieces of stone cut thin in standard-sized squares or rectangles and laid like tile. Durable and easy to care for, stone pavers have many of the same characteristics as ceramic floor tile. As with thick ceramic floor tiles, the weight of a stone or brick floor can be considerable, so the joists, the supporting beams beneath the floor, may need to be reinforced with triangular braces. Often the joists under kitchens have been cut or drilled to make way for water pipes and thus weakened.

While floor tiles are often a solid color, they do come in a variety of patterns, which can help to mask everyday dirt. The trellis-patterned tile with shiny glaze is an easy-care choice for the large kitchen **above**. An added detail is the use of tile against the base of the cabinet in the kick space. In a mix of several small patterns, a wall tile is used for the backsplash, another pattern is used for curtains, and in a dramatic gesture, still another pattern is used for the walls and ceiling.

When working with solid tiles, you have the option of creating your own floor pattern. **At right**, very durable 2-inch (5cm) unglazed commercial tiles are laid on the diagonal in an interesting design of only three colors: gray, black, and white. These tiles are available as single pieces or mounted on mesh sheets

Because they come from the earth, stone flooring materials come in their natural colors. Granite runs from grays, blacks, tans, and browns to reds and a color called plum. Marble has an even greater variety of tones and many types of veining and patterns. Slate can be black, dark green, rust red, or gray, like that used for both floor and countertop in the beautifully tailored kitchen **below**, where the pavers are laid in a staggered row like basket weave with a gray grout line in between. Also of interest in this kitchen is the large stainless steel sink with a drain board on each side, a practical echo of early kitchens.

© Jennifer Levy

LIGHTING

Since the kitchen is a working space that frequently doubles as a tranquil space for dining, it must incorporate two types of lighting: task lighting and general lighting. A third aspect of lighting is its decorative effect, which can be incorporated into the task and general lighting with dimmers and adjustable light sources. Long gone is the kitchen with a single ceiling fixture in the middle of the room, with your shadow falling on the counter in front of you no matter where you moved. With the many types of fixtures and bulbs that are now available, the lighting of the cooking and dining areas can make these activities much more pleasant and make the room seem more comfortable and attractive.

TASK LIGHTING AND GENERAL LIGHTING

Each work center in the kitchen, including the sink and the food-preparation areas, should be directly lit from above. Lights can be installed under the upper cabinets, hung on the wall, placed on or recessed in the ceiling, or hung on pendants. Venting hoods that go directly over the burners often contain a lighting fixture that is sealed in an easy-to-clean housing, and light fixtures can also be placed on either side of the cooktop or stove to avoid most of the cooking spatter and smoke. Lighting should always be installed with shades or directed in such a way that it is not aimed directly at your face. Wall-hung fixtures and pendants should be hung low enough that you cannot see the bare bulb beneath the shade.

General lighting encompasses the rest of the kitchen, including the walls, cabinets, and floors. To make cleaning easier, general lighting should be bright enough to reach far corners and into the interiors of open cabinets. Daylight flooding a kitchen from windows, glass doors, or skylights is the ideal light to work in. However, since most people prepare the major meal of the day and entertain after dark, general lighting is also necessary. In a contemporary kitchen, the lighting fixtures can be industrial-looking, with sockets, bulbs, and wiring exposed. In an old-fashioned kitchen, the lighting, though technically modern, will be concealed behind cabinets, recessed in the ceiling, or disguised with traditional shades.

Under-Cabinet Lighting

Fluorescent tube lighting is economical and particularly well suited to installation in long runs under cabinets. The light is bright, and although it usually has a slightly bluer cast than incandescent light, this "cold" look can be countered by warm white fluorescent tubes. Incandescent or tungsten bulbs, the standard egg-shaped light bulbs, emit a redder light that feels warmer and makes the room seem more cozy; tungsten showcase bulbs are tube-shaped and can be installed under cabinets. Miniature track lighting using tiny reflector bulbs or halogen bulbs are other choices for this confined space. Under-cabinet fixtures are usually installed toward the front of the cabinet with the light shining down and back toward the wall and backsplash.

© Jennifer Lévy

Ceiling Lighting

Recessed, surface-mounted, or track lighting fixtures provide task lighting from the ceiling. Recessed fixtures come in two sizes and use either spot or flood lamps. Spot lamps concentrate the light into a small area, whereas flood lamps cast a larger circle for more general lighting. A row of small recessed fixtures with small bulbs will create the most even light and not be very noticeable on the ceiling. Surface-mounted fixtures need some sort of shade to diffuse the light and reduce glare. Track lighting systems offer great flexibility and a variety of bulb and shade types. Low-voltage systems require a transformer and more expensive bulbs but are cooler to operate and use less electricity; a 50-watt low-voltage bulb can be substituted for a conventional 150-watt reflector flood bulb. Ceiling lighting aimed at the cabinets, walls, and countertops will combine task lighting and general lighting.

Four types of lighting illuminate the contemporary kitchen **at upper right**. Under-cabinet lighting is reflected off the granite backsplash and counter. Even though this lighting stops at either side of the cooktop, the area is still brightly lit. Individual ceiling fixtures shine down on the sink and the island at center, and track lighting is used to wash the walls and cabinets with general light. Finally, a suspended fixture with an etched shade lights the top of the dining table. Decorative lighting has not been forgotten in this kitchen: dimmers allow the kitchen area to become more subdued during evening meals.

The kitchen **at right** is lit by a skylight by day and recessed ceiling fixtures by night. Wall-hung fixtures inside the skylight well replace the natural light after the sun goes down, and task lighting is provided by concealed fixtures under the cabinets. When planning a kitchen, don't forget that the color of the countertops affects the amount of light required for work areas; dark-colored countertops absorb light and require higher wattage or more coverage than white surfaces such as these.

Wall Lighting

Wall-hung fixtures can provide both general and task lighting. Old-fashioned, candle-style sconces reproduce the glow of candlelight and are effective for dining. Wall-hung brackets with shades direct task light downward onto work surfaces. A small swivel lamp with a halogen bulb hung in a dark corner will brighten the area and make it usable. And fan-shaped wall sconces wash light upward onto the wall and ceiling for soft, general lighting.

Pendant Lighting

Pendants, lights suspended from the ceiling or track systems, provide countertop lighting in areas free of cabinets. With a slope adapter, a pendant can even be hung from a slanting cathedral ceiling. A pendant should be installed to hang low enough to avoid glare and prevent you from seeing the bulb. A

© Bill Rothschild, Designer: Denise Balassi

standard bulb with the end silvered reflects light back up under the shade and creates a soft, diffused effect.

Enameled metal industrial lamps, photographer's aluminum reflectors, and glass cone-shaped shades like those in the renovated barn kitchen on page 21 are practical and inexpensive fixtures. Traditional pendants include chandeliers in brass, iron, or crystal, and are most practical in the dining area, as they require space and provide only soft lighting. In the airy, high-ceilinged kitchen **on page 62**, pendant fixtures focus attention at eye level. Against the rear wall a dropped soffit creates a lower ceiling over the countertop and open shelves; unobtrusive recessed lights in the soffit shed light on and through the wire shelves and counter and light up that end of the kitchen at night. Pale pine furnishings, with the wall covering and ceramic tiles of the same warm, neutral color, form the perfect backdrop for food and flowers.

Table and Floor Lamps

Table and floor lamps, essentially portable, fill in where built-in lighting is lacking. A small table lamp tucked in between platters on a Welsh dresser will shed light on a nearby table. Or a floor lamp near a wing chair in the sitting area of a large kitchen can offer reading light and a homey atmosphere.

Decorative Lighting

Display lighting that highlights glassware, collections of china, or artwork can take a merely functional kitchen to another level, making it an interesting, even exciting place for the cook and guests. A small spotlight mounted on the kitchen ceiling track and aimed at a large basket of fruit on the counter will give it the effect of a piece of sculpture. Picture lights over prints or paintings on the wall will draw attention to them and provide background light for dining. Adding lights to the interior of glass-doored cabinets transforms patterned dinnerware into a decorative focus.

YOUR KITCHEN PLAN

Whether completely new construction, substantial renovation, or just a minor face-lift is in order, once your design thoughts are collected, your clipping file is full, and your practical needs are established, you can get down to the actual business of planning a kitchen. Even if you will be working with a professional—a kitchen designer, an architect, an interior designer, or a designer-contractor—you will be best served by having all your ideas formulated in advance. The professional consultant can then adapt your thoughts to a workable plan and, in reviewing your list of priorities, will be prompted to add solutions of his or her own. When building a new house, you will be able to expand or alter the overall space for the kitchen to accommodate all your ideas. Before construction starts is the time to refine your requirements and, like the pieces of a puzzle, fit them into a final plan. Even though it seems premature, this is the time to consider where to put the electrical outlet for the toaster and how much space will be taken up by the dishwasher door when it is open. In a renovation or simpler kitchen fix-up, it will take even more juggling to fit everything into the space you already have. Plan ahead.

PRIORITIES

Your kitchen planning will take several forms. The first project is to make a list of priorities, including what you expect to do in the kitchen and how you will use it. An informal family forum with one person writing down the ideas is a good way to start. In a group brainstorming session the ideas, hopes, and fantasies of everyone involved will have the chance to be aired. The wish list at this point may seem unwieldy, but it can be pared back later. You may not end up with a jukebox and Dad's entire collection of 45s, but the question of what kind of sound system to install will be considered. Children may come up with far-out cravings for their own fast-food department, so plan for a refrigerator with a large, accessible freezing compartment and locate the microwave nearby. The logic of kids is worth noting, too. They may have thoughts on how to streamline kitchen activities and where they will do homework and watch TV. You can discuss it all.

At this point the clipping file can be consulted to remind you of earlier ideas or to prompt new ones. Condense the clipping file to a list so all the random thoughts are in one place. Although it may seem complicated to do, it is much easier to cross items off a piece of paper now than to issue expensive change-work orders to the contractor later. If your meeting of the minds begins to falter, consult the list of activities below to prompt more detailed discussion.

Kitchen Activities

Jot down on your list the number of cooks in the family and the type of cooking that is done. How many cooks will use the kitchen at one time? Is one person making salad while another stirs the sauce on the cooktop? Is there a baker in the family who will need a place to knead the dough, let it rise, and an oven big enough to bake a week's supply at one time? These are the kinds of questions that will affect the final kitchen plan. Consider ethnic family traditions. Those who make pasta from scratch need a rack to dry it on. Swedish cookie makers need storage for cookie trays and cooling racks. Chinese cooking with a steamer or wok requires a stove top surrounded by easy-to-clean walls and a ventilating hood to draw off oily smoke. A kosher kitchen adhering to religious precepts entails separate areas for preparation of different types of food, including two sinks, two cutting areas, and two dishwashers. A family of vegetarians will require more preparation space near the sink; perhaps even a second sink for washing vegetables would be most efficient.

The question of work centers, areas designed for a particular task, can be discussed at this point, and will be referred to again when the list is transferred to a floor plan. A typical work center for beverages would include teapots and coffeemakers, counter space, storage for cups and mugs, sugar, honey, creamer and sugar bowl, spoons, napkins, filters, and perhaps a tray to serve from. All this may be near the sink or the stove. You may want a special place to sit and make grocery lists while consulting cookbooks or recipe files to make this task more pleasant. Make little tasks that are repeated often easier to perform in your new kitchen by including them on your list now: making toast, wash-ing vegetables and lettuce, thawing frozen foods, boiling water for pasta, making sandwiches, vacuuming the floor. Later these thoughts will prompt ideas for convenient storage for the tools and ingredients required by each activity.

Dining and Entertaining How a family gathers for meals and what kind of entertaining they do will affect the plan of a kitchen of any size, even the smallest. Consider each meal, starting with breakfast. Do you all sit down at once or does Mom or Dad get up early, have breakfast, and then get dressed while everyone else is in the kitchen? Maybe a stool at the kitchen counter would encourage a more leisurely morning meal.

Lunch these days may be only a weekend occurrence, but it can be a most enjoyable occasion. Comfortable chairs around a table in a sunny spot for an informal, relaxed meal in the kitchen may be the highlight of a quiet weekend. The attendant baskets, coolers, and Thermoses needed for picnics require quite a bit of storage space, but if they are easy to get at you might pack pic-nic lunches or suppers more often. Frequent outdoor dining in warm climates might prompt a deck or patio addition at the same time you remodel the kitchen. Even if this is not in the budget now, discuss it anyway. You may want to allow space for a door to the backyard even if the deck or patio won't be built until next year.

Dinner, the main meal and gathering time for most modern families, is probably the most important. The kitchen in new homes is usually part of a large space that includes dining and sitting areas. In older homes, kitchen space can be remodeled to annex the space of adjoining smaller rooms or expanded into the former dining room. Factors to consider are the number of people, the size of the table, the number of chairs, and the prox-imity to the kitchen work areas. Does the cook want to carry on a conversation with the rest of the family in the dining area? Or maybe you would prefer the dining room to be separate; this would be unusual now in the last decade of the twentieth cen-tury, but personal priorities are the most important. Since dinner-time is after dark through the winter months, be sure to consider ideas for lighting.

If your kids often bring friends home for dinner, the dining area may need to be flexible, with a table large enough to accommodate a couple of extra places. Extra leaves can be added or unfolded or an extra table set up. Adult evening entertaining may be limited to dinner for four, six, or eight, or there may be a crowd. If you really love to have lots of people, try to set down the maximum number you will entertain on your planning list. Do you have impromptu informal suppers or detailed menus and lengthy preparation? Even if you plan to do your entertaining buffet-style, you will still need storage space for dinnerware and flatware. Our entertaining patterns change over the years with the amount of time and money we can spend, where we live, and the local customs. Think about the future. If you plan to retire soon you may have more time to entertain.

Relaxation

The concept of the kitchen as a great room or medieval hall filtered through the home magazines during the opulent 1980s. Developed from the family room/kitchen combination, this modified form of the kitchen will probably continue, providing a space large enough for cooking and eating areas as well as a small living area for sofa and chairs. In many homes this living area will take the place of a separate living room; it should, therefore, be comfortable, an attractive yet relaxing room, where you can entertain and still put your feet up after a long day. Perhaps a fireplace or wood-burning stove can be included in the plan. Is this the most convenient spot for the television, VCR, and a sound system? Consider where you will put storage pieces, armoires, entertainment centers for equipment, table linens, and children's games. Bookcases may be needed and would give the dining area the look of a library. If space is limited, the dining table could be surrounded by large upholstered chairs that would take the place of living room furniture. Check your clipping file for all the options that you have liked and include them on the list.

Do your kids do their homework in the kitchen area? If so, it may help to include the computer or other homework aids on your list as well. If this room is to become the place to do homework, good lighting over the table and chairs the right height for writing will be required.

Equipment and Storage

Major and minor appliances are discussed in chapter 2. Run through the chapter and your appliance clipping file to make a list of what you want and need. Include the dimensions, the width, depth, and height at the front and back of each appliance. You can order appliance catalogs directly from the manufacturer or ask for photocopies of the catalog pages giving all dimensions and specifications at your local dealer.

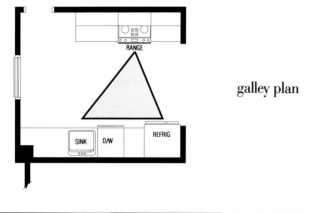

galley plan

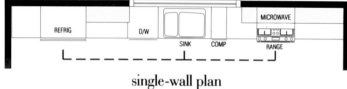

single-wall plan

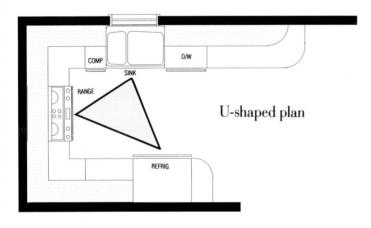

U-shaped plan

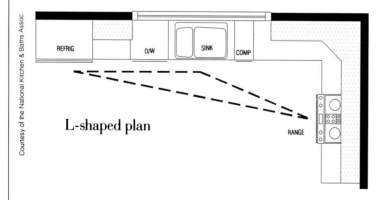

L-shaped plan

Courtesy of the National Kitchen & Baths Assoc.

Family food-storage needs vary depending upon eating and cooking habits. Large families depend much more on freezer storage than families of only two or three. Consider whether a larger refrigerator/freezer should go on your list. Another option you may want to consider is sealed storage space for grains, rice, and cereals to help them stay fresh longer. Keeping such items in glass jars is a practical and decorative solution.

Pots and pans take up the most kitchen space; a large stockpot can even occupy a whole cupboard. A rack hanging from the ceiling or on a wall, or an arrangement like the one **on page 69**, is an attractive option. Make two lists of pots and pans: one for those you use every day and one for those that are needed infrequently, such as a lobster steamer. The latter can be stored in a pantry, closet, or even in the attic, until needed.

Utensils are small but will need a drawer, a place on the wall, or space on the counter. Will you store your knives in a drawer, beyond the reach of children, or on a wall-mounted knife rack? Plan for stove-related utensils, such as wooden spoons, ladles, spatulas, and tongs, to be stored next to the stove. Towel bars and hooks for pot holders may seem unimportant now, but having them handy will make the kitchen operate much more smoothly. Add them to the list.

You will also need enough shelf and drawer space for a complete set of dinnerware, glassware, and flatware. Ideally, all of these things should be kept midway between the dishwasher and the table. Extra pieces, such as serving platters and dishes, also need to be listed but can go outside the kitchen if they are not used often.

THE FLOOR PLAN

Now that you have a long list with everything on it, you are ready for the floor plan. If you are turning the job over to a consultant, you can just pass on a copy of your list. However, if your clipping file includes interesting kitchen layouts with peninsulas, islands, and adjacent storage pantries or closets, you may want to

© image/dennis krukowski, Designer: Spottswood/Byron

pipes or ducts, and existing wiring, which you must take into consideration in your plan. You can save a lot of money if you are able to avoid moving or changing the services already there. Once you have the outline of your room on paper, fill in the pipes, ducts, and chimney flues that are obvious to you and try to figure where the hidden ones might be. Try tracing these lines from the basement so you know where they are located and mark them on the plan.

Galley, Single-Wall, U-shaped, L-shaped, Islands, and Peninsulas

Kitchens are generally rectilinear overall, but within that shape there are several layouts that have proven practical over time. The smallest kitchen—called the galley, as on a boat—consists of a narrow rectangle with cabinets and appliances on each side and just enough space down the middle for one or two people. A wider version of the galley has cabinets and counters down both sides of the room with access from one or either end. If well-planned, even a tiny galley kitchen can be efficient. The sophisticated work space **at left**, clad in dark gray matte plastic laminate, is an example of such a kitchen. The extra shelves at the end of the galley provide a shallow space for eating and storage for pots and pans above. The stainless steel appliances and fittings are easy to care for and add shiny chic to a minimal city space.

A single-wall kitchen has all the appliances and cabinets lined up along one wall. This arrangement works well in loftlike, open spaces where the kitchen is confined to one wall. The U-shaped kitchen has counter and cabinets across the end as well as the two side walls, providing the greatest countertop area in a small space. The U-shaped kitchen can be taken one step further to a full rectangle or square with cabinets and counters on all four sides, leaving space only for a door. The L-shaped plan consists of cabinets and counters down one long side of the room with a short return at one end. Sometimes the return at the end is a

sketch out a rough plan to show exactly what you want. If you are thinking of expanding your existing kitchen into other rooms, measure all the areas and draw a plan. There are kits available from kitchen and cabinet manufacturers to make this task easier, or you can use 1/4-inch (6.25mm) graph paper and allow one square per foot (0.3m) for a scale of 1/4 inch equals 1 foot. This will be a small plan but adequate for a general layout that shows placement of appliances.

In a remodeling project there will be permanent structural elements, such as chimneys, plumbing and waste lines, heating

© Phillip H. Ennis

island contains a bar sink, trash compactor, extra counter space, storage, and a cooktop without looking too bulky. Around the perimeter of the room such period treasures as a grandfather clock remain in their original positions.

The outline of your new kitchen space will dictate one of the plans listed above. Draw in the general outlines of cabinets and countertops, then read on about the work triangle and the arrangement of major appliances before you add them to your floor plan.

THE WORK TRIANGLE

Efficiency experts have worked out a simple plan to ensure that kitchen layouts will require a minimum number of steps for the cook. According to this formula, the cooktop, sink, and refrigerator must be arranged in a triangle. The shorter and more equal the legs of the triangle, the less walking the cook will have to do to carry things from the refrigerator to the sink to the cooktop. Because they are used less often, ovens are often placed just outside the triangle. However, since the microwave oven is likely to be used for many quick tasks and is relatively small, it can and should go within the triangle.

Now add the refrigerator, range, and sink to your floor plan. For the most economical arrangement, place the sink near the existing waste and supply plumbing lines so that they will not have to be moved or replaced. Since the refrigerator is massive and deeper than the countertop, it often works best at the end of the counter area. This begins the juggling phase of your design. Once these large items are sketched in, you will see how much counter space you will have and where you can locate the dishwasher, ovens (if separate from the range), microwave oven, food processor, and so on down the line to the smallest items. This step may necessitate moving the sink a little to the right or left, shifting the range so there is room for the oven door to open, or making other similar adjustments.

peninsula that is only counter high and functions as a divider between the cooking and eating areas.

The kitchen island is the modern version of the old kitchen worktable. It is located in the center of the single-wall, U-shaped, or L-shaped kitchen and is an excellent way to add counter space, a sink, or a cooktop. Islands are often made of standard cabinets, sometimes supplemented with bookshelves or an eating counter. They can also be configured in nonstandard ways to get the best use of available space, like the new island in the middle of the traditional room **above**, which provides a practical kitchen update without disturbing the windows or walls. This

Work Centers and Storage

The areas to either side of the sink, refrigerator, and cooktop are the sites of the most concentrated activity in the kitchen. Experts recommend a range of counter lengths for these areas. There should be at least 18 inches (45cm) and ideally 36 inches (96cm) on either side of the sink for food preparation, dishwashing, and cleanup. Over the dishwasher, to the right or left of the sink, you will need 24 inches (60cm) of counter space. And there should be at least 18 to 24 inches (45 to 60cm) on either side of a cooktop for preparing foods for cooking. If there is countertop on one side of the cooktop only, provide at least 36 inches (96cm) and ideally up to 42 inches (105cm) of counter. This measurement is understandable, as you do not want to be crowded when removing lids or hot pans from the burners. There should also be at least 16 inches (40cm) next to the handle side of the refrigerator for putting away groceries and wrapping and storing refrigerated foods. Of course, the more counter space, the better.

© Tim Lee

Adjust your plan to include adequate counter space. Although you may be tempted to get away with less, you will find the actual kitchen even more confining than it looks on paper. When in doubt, try out the measurements in your existing kitchen to be sure. If you have visited a kitchen that seemed especially comfortable, ask to take measurements and compare them to your plan. If you are working with a professional designer's plans, you may want to compare them to an existing kitchen to get a feeling for the dimensions.

The structure of your kitchen is growing on paper. Now add the storage areas, upper cabinets, and pantry closets and define how the lower cabinets will be used. Provide storage space near the work centers for each activity: for pots and pans near the range, for washing and cleaning materials near the sink, and for dinnerware near the dishwasher.

Electricity, Lighting, and Ventilation

The electrical and ventilation systems are the invisible elements in your plan, but because they may affect where you can or cannot put things they should be included. For instance, duplex receptacles (outlets) may have to be moved to the wall above the countertop within reach of countertop appliances. The duct for a venting hood over the range requires space in the wall cavity or on the wall behind a shallow cabinet. Now is a good time to sketch in lighting fixtures, switches, and dimmers so the electrician has a good idea of what you want. He can tell you where he can or cannot run wiring and how much space you have for recessed fixtures.

With your plan in hand, you can now talk to a kitchen consultant, designer, architect, or contractor, confident with the knowledge that you have thought out your ideas to the best of your ability. With all this information on paper and fresh in your mind, you will have a much easier time communicating your ideas and will be better able to understand the suggestions made by the experts. Good luck and bon appétit!

part two

WALLS AND WINDOWS

COLOR AND PATTERN

Anyone who has come up with a decorating idea for the home and then seen it through to completion can recall that rush of satisfaction, that pleasure derived from the process of change. For most of us, the interior walls of our homes are the largest areas we will ever have to work with to express our sense of style and satisfy our personal creativity. There is an infinite variety of ways to change a room through the styling of the walls. Sometimes it is just a new coat of paint in the same color that gives a room a fresh aspect. A change in color, pattern, or texture can alter the purpose of a space, how it functions, and the mood it imparts. For instance, a small, dark room used for viewing television can easily be transformed into a bright breakfast spot. Color on the walls in clear tints and light tones will make the room seem cheerier and set the stage for the furniture, whether Victorian wicker or Scandinavian modern in style.

Developing the scheme for a room, the style and mood, is exciting and fun. Looking for ideas, colors, and patterns can be a treasure hunt, taking you through museums, designer showcase houses, decorating magazines, the room settings in home furnishings stores, and the pages of books. It is a very good idea to start a clipping file that includes pictures of rooms published in magazines, Polaroids of ideas in stores or friends' homes, and paint chips and wallcovering and fabric swatches. At the beginning of your quest for ideas, small samples that are free from the paint store and small pieces of fabric are all that are necessary. Later, once the general style and mood are established, larger samples will be needed to be sure the scale and overall color are what you expected. The new combinations you will concoct using all the elements you have found will come together in unusual and personal ways and will inspire the next phase, the execution of your scheme. Whether you do it yourself or oversee the work of contracted professionals or craftsmen, the real thrill will be in the day-to-day process, right up to the grand finale: your finished room.

Color has a great impact on the style and mood of a room. Flipping through a paint-color book or perusing the racks of color in the paint store, one would suppose that every shade, tint, or tone is there for the buying. However, trying to match the background of a wallpaper print or the color of a fabric, or just coming up with the shade you have in your mind's eye, often results in the realization that the exact color you need will have to be mixed. When putting together your scheme, take home a range of colors, including shades that are darker and lighter, and bluer, redder, and more yellow than your first choice. These colors will be altered by the light in the room, differing in daylight or by artificial light at night. They will also be affected by the other colors you use in the room. For example, red curtains in a yellow room will make the walls glow with a pinkish cast. An olive green wall will appear greener at night under yellow incandescent light. The best way to know how a color will look is to tape samples to the wall in the intended room and leave them there for a day or two. Look at them from time to time, in the morning, afternoon, and evening. Also include samples of fabrics and wallcoverings that you may consider for your scheme and compare these with your existing furniture and curtain fabrics.

Patterns in wallcoverings and fabrics will look different from across the room than they do in your hand. The colors in small overall patterns will blend together at a distance to form a third color. For instance, a fine blue-and-red stripe can look lavender or violet. Some stores will loan fabric and wallpaper books so you can take them home. If samples are not available, you may consider buying a yard (meter), especially if it contains a large-scale pattern, to be sure of its effect in the actual room. This initial expense will be worth the assurance that you have chosen the right pattern and color.

© Phillip H. Ennis

EFFECTS OF COLOR

There are general rules about the effects of color on walls. Lighter colors make a room seem larger, whereas darker colors bring the walls closer and make a room seem smaller. Warm colors, those based on red and yellow tones, feel warmer and cozier and are suggested for rooms on the north or cool side of a building. Cool colors, blues and greens, are often used in south-facing rooms that receive a lot of sunlight. Reds are supposed to be exciting and make your blood pressure rise, while greens are considered the most relaxing and the easiest on the eyes. The colors rose, pink, and peach are thought to flatter complexions and are suggested for rooms destined for entertaining and for dressing and bathing areas.

In the traditional room **above**, which has been painted and glazed shiny red, the deep color makes the room seem smaller and more intimate. It exudes a most relaxing, inviting warmth. Black shades on the lamps subdue the artificial light and aim it down onto the desktop and on the upholstery of the chaise longue, with its red woolen throw. The secondary color, slate blue, is gently repeated with red in the curtains, the rug, and the Chinese export porcelain on the mantelpiece.

Flat black, the ultimate dark color, provides the drama of nighttime city living **at right**. This foyer contains carefully balanced furnishings placed on either side of a handsome neoclassical desk. Equally deliberate are the paired black urns, the gleaming brass candle brackets, and the centered print with black mat and gilded frame. Although contrived, the final effect is sophisticated and arresting, a visual pleasure to homeowner and visitor alike.

Quite the opposite, yet heeding the same call for drama, is the all-white room with a striking antique mirror **at right**. The monochromaticity of the creamy, off-white carpet, walls, bedspread, and upholstered chair creates a pale, peaceful retreat, simple in detail yet rich in design. This room illustrates how colors in a monochromatic scheme need not match exactly. The carpet is a bit more yellow than the walls, and the chair is covered in a muslin-color cloth rather than one that is stark white. In addition, the colors are affected by texture, with light absorbed by the softer materials and reflected off the smooth surfaces to create still lighter highlights.

© Eric Roth; Design: Veronique Louvet

© Courtesy of John Widdicomb Company

Paint can be used to mask or enhance architectural details and can be an inexpensive way to handle a feature that, depending on its nature, might otherwise be problematic or unappreciated. For instance, to hide architectural flaws or exposed pipes, paint them the same color as the walls, and they will blend in and be much less noticeable. On the other hand, to highlight beautiful trim, paint it a contrasting color, as was done in the traditional home **on the upper left-hand corner of page 80**, where yellow walls are framed with white moldings and trim. The contrast makes a light but rich setting for the antique furnishings. This yellow is strong, almost egg yolk in hue, with red-orange tones rather than green ones. Yellows can be tricky and must be tried in daylight and by lamplight at night. Greener yellows look bright by day but fade and seem grayer at night.

higher and makes the room appear more spacious; the under-eaves cupboard, painted to match the walls, seems unobtrusive. The lacey pattern of hand-painted foliage, birds, and flowers is reminiscent of the wallpapers imported from the Orient in the early nineteenth century. Furnishings from the American Federal period are also appropriate here even though the room has a decidedly nontraditional air.

The accepted rules of decor suggest small patterns for small rooms and large patterns for large rooms. Patterns with a shared coloration may be mixed successfully if they are of different scales. In the creative world of design, however, rules can also be broken with great results.

MIXING COLORS

For some people mixing colors is almost second nature. They choose articles of clothing, arrange flowering plants in the garden, and set their dinner tables with seeming abandon, swiftly combining colors and patterns into coordinated, exciting

EFFECTS OF PATTERN

Pattern can also affect your perception of a room. Small patterns will blur together into a quiet background, while large patterns will demand notice. A room with many angles, dormers, and low-hanging eaves can be expanded by using the same pattern on both walls and ceiling. A very large room can be made more interesting by breaking large expanses of wall with a chair rail and using different patterns above and below it. Wall areas can also be defined with wallpaper or stenciled borders. The dominant color in a pattern will affect the visual size and shape of a room: a light color will make it seem larger and a dark color will seem to diminish the space.

In the bedroom under the eaves **at right**, mossy green delineates the raised panel woodwork and trim. The lighter green background on the walls and ceiling makes them seem even

80

schemes that catch the eye. Others need to find inspiration in the things around them. Nature is a good source for color combinations. Look out the window on a summer day and observe the many shades of green: tree leaves are dark green, grass is a range of emerald to lime color, and the new leaves of daylilies are even more yellow. Since green is made up of two primary colors, blue and yellow, any of these greens will go together. However, if you are starting with a teal green, which is a blue-green, you will find that it will go best with other colors that have a blue cast, for instance, a pink with some blue in it rather than a peachy pink. The primaries red and blue mixed together make purple, and red mixed with yellow makes orange. If you have never mixed paint colors, spend an hour with a children's watercolor or poster color set to see how colors affect each other. You'll find, for example, that adding white will make a lighter tint, while adding black will make a darker, grayer shade.

Sticking with several shades of one color is a safe and very effective way to combine color. If you wish to be more adventurous, try two or three different colors. An excellent guide to color combinations is the colors chosen for printed fabrics. The professional colorists who decide on the different color ways for each pattern have a deep understanding of how colors affect each other and how they will look together. If you have chosen a fabric pattern, use its colors as a guide for other colors in the room. The wall paint, carpet color, curtains, and accessories can all be chosen from the printed fabric without fear of making a color mistake. Be aware that the finish on a fabric or on a painted or papered wall can alter a color. A glossy finish will make the color seem more intense, while a flat finish will seem velvety and soft, making the color more diffused.

Colors of strong contrast used together will create a much more lively scheme than a monochromatic combination of shades of all one color. In the room **at upper right**, in a reversal of the rules, blue walls recede under red damask drapery and a brilliant yellow cornice. Your attention is drawn to the gilded mirror and artwork, which float against the deep back-

© Phillip H. Ennis

ground, and to the bright yellow upholstery of the arm and side chairs. The boldly patterned rug, the casual arrangement of furniture, and the many small tables add up to an eclectic design with Edwardian overtones.

Unusual combinations of patterns and colors will work well together if there is a unifying thread, such as a pattern theme from one design style or a common color. Be lavish in your collection of samples and try out all the possible combinations. Try the combinations that seem unusual or impossible, too. You may be surprised and end up with colors and patterns that you never expected to work. The proof is in the doing, and the final judgment is up to you. If you like the scheme, consider it successful.

chapter two

PAINT

P aint is the quickest and easiest way to change a room. Early paints were mixed by the painter from packets of dry pigments, but when premixed paints came on the market in the 1870s, consumers gained the freedom to choose from color chips or samples. More and more colors have been made available over the years, with different colors becoming popular in different eras. With more sophisticated analysis of historic paint samples developed recently, it was discovered that the colors used in the eighteenth century were much brighter and more intense than previously thought. Historic restorations no longer feature faded, grayed colors, but now use emerald green, bright red, turquoise blue, and orange the color of pumpkins. Colors were light early in the nineteenth century and then became increasingly dark as the Victorian era progressed. Deep rose-reds, ocher yellow-golds, and shades of lavender became popular. With the current interest in historically accurate colors, manufacturers have developed color ranges appropriate to these periods. If you cannot find the exact color among paint manufacturers' chips, paint store proprietors will be able to custom-match paint to any sample you bring in. In some paint stores, new computerized equipment can analyze a color swatch and provide the formula for mixing that color.

Paint comes in several finishes: flat (or matte), eggshell, satin, semigloss, and high gloss. The flat finish is best for walls and ceilings where there is little direct contact with hands. Eggshell and satin paints have a soft sheen and are good choices for covering staircase walls, kitchens, and bathrooms because they can be gently wiped clean. Semigloss and high gloss are recommended for door and window trim as they repel water and can be washed. The glossier the surface, the more durable the paint. However, semi- and high-gloss paint will accentuate the texture of the wall surface, making any unevenness or bumps much more obvious. To visually smooth out a rough wall surface, use a flat paint.

Paints generally come in two varieties: alkyd (oil-based) or latex (water-based). The former is thinned using turpentine or mineral spirits, the latter using water. Oil paint was once the choice of professional painters, but now, because of the toxic volatile organic compounds (VOCs) in oil paints, fewer oil-based flat paints are available for interior application. At the same time, latex paints have improved in quality over the years, are easy to apply, and come in endless ranges of color. In addition, brush cleanup with water-based paint is much easier and less toxic to the painter than with oil-based paints. For the best finish with latex paint, apply a coat of oil-based primer over any previous paint layers and then finish with one or two top coats of latex. Newly developed acrylic and acrylic epoxy paints are also water-based and easy to apply.

When walls are in particularly bad condition, they may need to be replastered with a skim or finish coat of plaster before being painted. In old houses where the plaster has cracked and/or pulled away from the lath beneath, it is possible to anchor it with plaster washers and then hang lining paper or canvas on the wall like wallpaper to help stabilize it. This lining can then be primed and painted as usual.

FANCY PAINTED FINISHES

To provide texture and depth to a painted wall, early itinerant housepainters developed some unusual techniques that have been revived and are often used today; they are often applied to furniture as well as walls. Many of these methods involve texturing the paint while it is still wet, using feathers, combs, sponges, or wadded-up rags or paper. Wood graining, or *faux bois* (French for "fake wood"), consists of brown paint over a tan coat, streaked and swirled to look like real wood, complete with knots. Through this method, plain pine woodwork and doors can be made to look like mahogany, rosewood, or walnut. The trim and cabinets in the butler's pantry **at right** take on a rustic air with *faux bois* worked in pale colors. Wallpaper in a tiny pattern of tan on moss green is the perfect foil for the wood tones and the collection of green and yellow majolica pottery. It is yellow, the common element in both the tan and green, that coordinates this color scheme and makes it work so well.

Faux marbre, or marbling, imitates the look of marble on floors, baseboards, and other woodwork. Veins of color are threaded through the wet paint with feathers or fine brushes. When dry, the marbling is varnished with polyurethane or acrylic varnish in a satin or high-gloss finish. Be aware that polyurethane yellows over time and will affect the color of the

© Bill Rothschild. Design: Tony Antine

paint beneath. New polymer varnish offers a harder finish than polyurethane and does not yellow, but it is more expensive.

Sponging and scumbling give an illusion of texture and depth to wall surfaces by combining two or three colors in an allover irregular pattern. In the small sitting room **on the upper left-hand corner of page 85**, yellow ocher has been sponged over a pale yellow base coat, giving the walls a sophisticated, beautiful texture. The table sports a marbled top achieved by drawing a feather through wet paint to form veins and by smudging several colors together to provide shading.

Walls can also be textured with sponges, rags, or combs using clear glaze that has been colored with universal tints or

© Eric Roth, Design: MJ Berries

© Eric Roth, Design: Toni Peabody

acrylic paints available at paint stores. Since glazes are translucent, they can be layered for a rich buildup of color. In the small study **at upper right**, red glaze over a pale tan background has been strieed by dragging a dry brush vertically down the wall. The result is very rich, with a gentle sheen, a fitting backdrop for the collection of photos, cards, and letters on this busy desk. In a similar technique, combed red paint is confined to stripes on a wall in the early country residence **at lower right**. Strips of masking tape outlined the areas, and then the paint was brushed on and immediately combed with a comb cut from a piece of flexible plastic. Clearly crude and decorative in a folk art manner, the stripes give structure to the arrangement of primitive paintings.

STENCILING

Although often thought of as the poor man's wallpaper, stenciling offers the greatest range of custom colors and patterns you can find. The base coat and the stencil can be simple, using

© Eric Roth, Pomegranate Inn

© Richard Mandelkorn

them the appearance of receding, making the room feel larger than it really is. Here, the pattern is confined to a large border at the base of the walls and a shallow band across the ceiling with scattered butterflies in between.

Stencils can be purchased precut in kits or traced from books of stencil designs. There are folk art designs of hearts, birds, and flowers that can be used as overall fields, borders, or stripes in country settings. Victorian stencils of enormous size can be combined in intricate patterns in many colors, including metallics of silver and gold. You can create your own designs by tracing a motif from a favorite wallpaper or fabric, or any other graphic source. Stencil designs may be enlarged or made smaller to suit the scale of a particular room. Use a photocopier to rescale the design, then use the photocopy as an underlay and cut the stencil in clear acetate. This flexible stenciling film is available at any art supply store, and it can be washed and reused many times.

only two colors, or they can add up to an intricate pattern of many colors that overlap and blend.

Stencils are often used to highlight an architectural detail. A chair rail can fill practical as well as decorative needs; it protects the wall from being bumped and scraped by chair backs and can also provide a base for a stenciled border, as in the hallway **above**. Flowers and swag stenciling combined with bands of deep green and red accent the graceful architecture of this sweeping staircase and add decorative formality to the limited wall space. The individual stencils allow for curves and customized spacing that would not be possible with preprinted wallpaper borders.

The effects you can achieve with stencils are amazingly varied, and their use should not by any means be limited to formal settings like the one above. A very soft pattern of foliage and scattered butterflies adds life to the pale walls **at right** and gives

Designer: Connie Beale, photo by Bill Stites

© Jennifer Lévy

SCENIC PAINTINGS

Painted scenes of the world have been applied to walls since the people of what is now Lascaux, France, painted pictures of their hunts for deer and buffalo on the walls of underground caves. Roman houses in the ancient towns of Pompeii and Herculaneum featured frescoes of garden and domestic scenes in brilliant colors, many of which were preserved by the ash of the nearby Mount Vesuvius. Frescoes are wall paintings where water-based paint is applied directly to damp plaster before it has cured. The paint is then absorbed by the plaster for a very long-lasting finish. In earlier times, itinerant artists in rural areas painted local scenes in the finer homes. Whether primitive or refined, these paintings changed the nature of the room from

an ordinary space into a total experience. Today, many artists are willing to take up a brush for a private commission. The homeowner with some talent and lots of self-confidence can do the same.

The wonderful landscape of hills, trees, and houses **above** transports guests at this table to another world and another era. Although primitive in spirit, the detail of the painting catches your eye and invites you to wander along the country roads, down to the edge of the lake to see the man sitting in a small boat. As can be seen in the mirror's reflection, the painting is confined between the crown molding at the top of the wall and the chair rail and is not blocked by any tall pieces of furniture.

© Bill Rothschild, Design: Becky Franco

thing. Shadows and the rendering of perspective make the cabinet seem three-dimensional and give the shelves depth. The candle sconces on either side are genuine, but what about the clock face on the middle shelf? That is a question that only time will answer.

Sometimes trompe l'oeil has a bit more basis in reality, making it even more deceptive. The large gilded mirror that is located in the palatial setting **below** becomes even more interesting with the addition of trompe l'oeil muntins painted on the

© Bill Rothschild, Design: Lee Ames

TROMPE L'OEIL

The type of wall painting known as trompe l'oeil, meaning "trick the eye," is so realistic that you often have to touch it to be sure it's not real. Used to create realistic focal points or vistas that visually open up a space, these designs usually incorporate an architectural element such as a door or window that is correct in scale and appropriate in location. This is the first part of the mental trick. The second part involves the use of details, such as curtains in the window, a hasty note pinned to a doorframe, or other little things that would be there in real life. **Above**, the French Provincial cabinet painted on the wall repeats the lines of the table and chairs in this room that is too small for the real

© Bill Rothschild, Design: Jeanne Leonard

glass and feathery vines trailing across the frame and onto the wall itself. A bird in flight and a dragonfly add to the fairy tale feeling that the mirror evokes, which is made even more eerie by the actual reflection of the room. Also of note in this room are the walls, which have a sponged paint finish. The golden glow of the wall color is especially effective with the gilded mirror frame and the marble doorframe and furniture.

Trompe l'oeil is not always so securely contained. A trellis added to the end of the living room **above** is the support for hand-painted wisteria and a visiting bird; the intention here is to make you think for a moment that it is the wall, rather than the wisteria, that does not really exist. The panels of the closet doors are outlined in the same yellow as the walls, breaking up the large expanse of white and continuing the tracery effect.

WALLCOVERINGS

Wallcoverings make the world of pattern and color almost instantly available. They also solve the problem of recurrent cracks in old plaster and can hide problem walls. Wallcoverings include wallpapers, metallics, vinyls, grass cloths, and other textures as well as fabrics that can be paper-backed and pasted up or stretched and stapled like upholstery. Wallcovering patterns are available in coordinated sets with grounds and borders in various sizes. In addition, coordinating fabrics in a variety of patterns and colors that are designed to go with the wallcoverings can be purchased at the same source. In some cases, curtains, shower curtains, bedspreads, and other ready-made accessories are also elements of the same design package. Be sure to pin up samples of wallcoverings for the intended room along with your choices of paint color for ceiling and woodwork to make sure everything works together. All the painting will be completed before the wallcovering is installed, so you must decide on both paint color and wallcovering pattern before the wallcovering is ordered.

WALLPAPER

The choice of wallcovering is going to have a great effect on the final scheme for the room. Patterns that are derived from particular periods will establish the room's style and atmosphere. For example, wallpapers based on the hand-blocked papers from the eighteenth century are extremely bold; some are flocked in imitation of expensive crimson velvet wallhangings, while others contain bold floral designs derived from brocade and printed dress fabrics of the time. Wallpapers of this period often incorporated large-scale architectural motifs of columns and arches. Some depicted classical ruins and others blocks of stone or marble in a trompe l'oeil effect. Toward the end of the eighteenth century, with the influence of the Adam brothers in England, design elements in wallpapers became lighter and more classical. Oval rosettes were combined with delicate floral swags in more subdued colors, many in shades of gray, black, and white. Paper panels block-printed by hand in France featured pastoral scenes with neoclassic motifs in up to eighty-five colors. These

decorate simple pieces of furniture. An arrangement of border and ground cut from leftover paper and laid on a chest of drawers or a table can be protected by a sheet of ¼-inch (6mm) glass cut to fit the top. The collage need not be glued down or permanent. A folding screen can take on architectural status when decorated with borders that are used elsewhere in the same room. Wallpaper borders can also be applied to painted walls; if the background color matches the paint, they can assume the character of a stenciled or hand-painted design.

FABRIC ON WALLS

Fabric can be pasted, stapled, or tacked to walls. Sheets and similar sturdy cottons with overall patterns can be glued with wallpaper paste directly to a wall that has been primed white. The white background is necessary, as another color might show through the fabric. Fabric can be stapled to walls with a staple gun, and the seams covered with flat braid or painted strips of wood lattice. To soundproof a room, first staple up polyester quilt batting and then cover it with fabric. Colored thumbtacks placed in rows through the fabric and batting will give the wall a tufted, quilted look. Professional upholsterers hang fabric on walls using traditional upholstery techniques. The seams of the fabric are sewn before installation, and the panels of fabric are tacked to wood frames that are attached to the walls.

In the converted porch at the back of a house **at left**, a large-patterned chintz is used lavishly on the walls, at the window, and on all the upholstered furniture. Pale green paint and a border of red gimp along the ceiling beams and around the trim establishes the framework for these fanciful furnishings. The bamboo and lacquer étagère is the focal point for china and flowers. Feel free to use lots of pattern, but also provide artwork or accessories that will catch the eye and relieve any potentially overwhelming sameness of design.

Walls can also be covered with fabric shirred or gathered on curtain rods. A second rod at the baseboard level will pull the fabric taut into vertical folds, or the bottom hem can be left hanging free. Padded, gathered, or free-hanging fabric wallcoverings will disguise cracked or badly patched walls and provide soundproofing. When thoughtfully arranged, draped fabric can become architecture, as in the room **below**, where creamy white fabric is gathered and stitched to small brass rings and hung from brass rods that encircle the room. A former doorway has been converted to a bookcase, and the curtain is simply pulled aside with brass hold backs. The same technique is used at working doorways and at the windows, eliminating the need for additional window treatments. The brass rods also function as picture molding so that artwork can hang freely in front of the drapery. A band of stenciling above the rod sets the classic theme for the rest of the French-style furniture.

Designer: Connie Beale, photo by Phillip H. Ennis

ARCHITECTURAL FINISHES

Although usually considered in terms of their practical function, building materials such as plaster, brick and stone, and wood paneling and molding add decorative interest to the interior walls of the home and should be considered early in the planning process. In new construction, these finishes will be installed by the carpenter or mason. However, most of these materials can also be applied to existing walls. Even stone, with its heavy, massive look, is available in thin sheets that can be fixed to the wall and then grouted much like ceramic tile. Architectural details such as built-in cabinets and bookcases also provide visual interest and line, and they have the added benefit of helping to solve the very real problems of storage. Another detail that must be considered when planning the design scheme of a room is the choice of artwork, which can enhance the visual impact of the walls perhaps more than any other elements.

PLASTER

Interior walls are usually finished in plaster or the modern equivalent, plasterboard or drywall, which consists of pressed gypsum plaster sheathed with paper. The plaster in old houses will have a rough or smooth finish depending on its period and style. Many homes have plaster textured with sand and troweled in circular swirls. The plaster in more expensive or more formal houses is harder and smoother, with a satiny sheen. Even though drywall is much easier to install, it does not have the same look as plaster, and restoration experts recommend saving as much original plaster as possible when renovating an old building. One type of drywall has a special paper finish that accepts a skim coat of finishing plaster and comes closer to looking like old-fashioned plaster. The plaster in European and South American homes is often tinted with color before application, and the surface textured or troweled smooth.

lines. Stone found in meadows or brooks and left in its natural shape is called fieldstone or rubble. Stone that is cut from a quarry and comes in neatly cut rectangles is called ashlar. There are many variations of the basic types of stone—granite, quartz, shale, slate, limestone, marble, and sandstone—in a wide variety of colors. The finish of the stone, whether it is cut smooth or left rough, can also vary and will affect the look of the finished wall. In the slick, contemporary kitchen **at left**, the wall is lined in rough-dressed sandstone set with gray mortar. The contrast of grays, from the rough stone to the satin-finished stainless steel, is very effective and makes a wonderful backdrop for food, fruit, and flowers. Brick and stone walls can be sealed with a clear coating to cut down on mortar dust and sand, but the sealer creates a "wet" look that may or may not be desirable.

Older buildings built of brick or stone usually have interior walls covered with plaster. Removing the plaster to expose the texture of these walls may not leave you with the best quality of brick or stonework, since the original mason expected it to be

BRICK AND STONE

A brick or stone wall, with its natural color, texture, and pattern, will impart its inherent character to a room. Because of their weight, such walls are usually confined to the exterior of a house; properly supported, they may be used as partition walls. Indeed, chimney walls of brick or stone can play an important part in the design of a new home, adding color and texture around the fireplace, which can be a major focus of everyday living. Interior walls of stone are often included in solar houses, where they serve as Trombe walls, absorbing and storing the heat of the sun.

New walls can be built of brick or stone in a range of types and colors. There are early handmade bricks, rather small and irregular in shape, and later machine-made bricks that have hard surfaces and are designed to be laid with very thin mortar

98

covered. Also, since it is the inside of an exterior wall that is exposed, this procedure is not always practical—it might require extensive repointing (filling the joints with mortar) to make the wall airtight. In cities where a brick wall is a common wall with the next building, this is not as much of a problem. You may decide that the interesting atmosphere provided by an old brick or stone wall may outweigh its drawbacks, as did the owners of the town house **at lower left**. Here the old brick wall is left rough with patches of mortar, a real contrast to the high-style furnishings. The feeling, however, is warm and relaxed, rather like being snug in a cave or wine cellar. You might also consider exposing the interior face of an old brick or stone chimney; if you live in a very old house, you may discover one buried in the walls when you undertake renovations.

WOOD PANELING

The mention of wood paneling conjures up images of elegant libraries, paneled drawing rooms, and on a more down-to-earth level, the mid-twentieth-century study or den. In seventeenth- and eighteenth-century France, fashionable men and women would retire from the royal court to a cabinet, a small private room where dining and entertaining were more intimate and informal. A far cry from what we call a cabinet today, there are some similarities. The walls were often wood lined, with carved moldings and inset panels, usually painted, which formed a box within a room. With the decline of the monarchy and the dissolution of large estates, these wooden rooms were often dismantled, sold, and reinstalled elsewhere. Salvage firms are now aware of the value of old wood paneling and are quick to rescue and resell individual pieces or whole rooms. An antique carved panel can be set into a new wall made by a carpenter that has been finished to match the old piece of woodwork.

Wood paneling can be very ornate and complex, or as simple as plain boards installed one next to the other. The best paneling is made with tongue-and-groove edges that slide together and

allow for the natural swelling and shrinking of the wood that occurs with changes in the weather. Tongue-and-groove edges also hide the nails used for installation. At the top of the price range are raised panels with crown moldings in hardwoods such as walnut, oak, cherry, or mahogany. A less costly wood is pine, although today clear pine is as expensive as some hardwoods. Complex paneling is sometimes painted, particularly if the wood from which it is made is not of top quality. In the sitting room **below**, raised wood panels set into a framework cover the chimney wall. The panels are continued beneath the chair rail around the other three walls. The flat finish is a pumpkin-colored milk paint that comes as a package of dry pigment, which you mix when you are ready to paint. The brushstrokes left on the surface of the paint add to the rustic, primitive quality.

© Eric Roth, Design: Rebecca Hathaway

or paint and then varnished to make maintenance easier. For a particularly rustic look, consider using rough-sawn wood or old barn siding to cover a wall.

BOOKCASES

One of humankind's better inventions is the basic bookshelf. Even in its simplest form of a few boards nailed together, the bookshelf incorporates storage with display in a way that converts possessions—books, photos, vases, and trophies—to visual assets. Books stored on shelves are much more likely to be read or referred to than those in a box in a closet. Dinnerware, platters, and covered dishes that are not used every day can be set in between sections of books and enjoyed for their colorful patterns and shapes. When small works of art are arranged on one shelf rather than scattered at large in a room, they become the center of attention. Lighting incorporated within the shelves can spotlight certain objects and allow other areas to fall into shadow. The architectural detail of the grand bookcase cabinet

Wainscoting usually refers to the paneled area underneath a chair rail. The room **above** illustrates another type of wainscoting: narrow strips of wood installed vertically on the walls and covering the ceiling. This wainscoting consists of tongue-and-groove strips with a V groove or a rounded bead down the middle and along each edge; these strips are available at any lumber yard and can be clear-finished or painted as desired. This type of wainscoting is often found in nineteenth-century American farmhouses. Note how in this kitchen, the oddly shaped chimney takes on new life with handmade ceramic tiles.

Woods with knots and flaws cost less and provide an informal, rustic look. Knotty pine boards with V grooves sheath the walls in the cottage dining room **at right**. Sealed with a clear varnish, these walls will darken with time to a deep honey-brown color. To keep it pale, wood can be pickled with a thin wash of white stain

© Phillip H. Ennis

on this page is highlighted by bands of ebony-stained molding on the pale wood veneer, which contrasts with the maroon-painted walls. The shelves are stained black, making books and objects seem to float in space. A classical arrangement of urns with a clock in the center section provides a formal focus for the whole unit. Bookcases can be formal or informal as fits the style of the room, but no matter how humble or grand, they can be only as attractive as the arrangement of their contents.

Bookcases can be freestanding or built in. If you are planning to move to another home in the near future, consider bookcases as pieces of furniture. A single unit at the center of a wall, a pair, or a row of three will have the same architectural impact as a built-in unit. Wall-hung shelves are practical over desks or worktables and if made the same width as the furniture beneath, will provide a custom look. If a room has odd-sized or -shaped areas, consider building in shelves to even out the architecture.

101

© Phillip H. Ennis

In city apartments, walls are often broken up by structural supports in the corners of rooms, and these walls can be made more streamlined by filling in the gaps with shelving. In a renovation project, new plumbing or ductwork is often run just under the ceiling along one wall. Boxing in the pipes with a new soffit and filling in the space beneath it with shelving is an excellent way to disguise and cure an awkward situation.

The color and finish of a bookcase or shelving should be considered in relation to the other design elements in the room. A contrasting color will make the unit stand out as a strong focus, like the ebony-trimmed blond bookcase on page 101. Tall bookcases are striking due to their size and may dominate the rest of a scheme. Painting a bookcase the same color as the woodwork or wall will make it less obtrusive, or if it is freestanding, help it to appear built-in. A little detail that can make a bookcase quite special is the use of paint or fabric of a coordinating color inside the shelves on the back wall.

A bookcase that is just a flight of shelves need be only 10 inches (25cm) deep and will not take up much floor space. Deeper units with cabinets or drawers in the base offer a greater variety of storage. Televisions, VCRs, and audio equipment require different shelf depths. Most TVs are at least 17 inches (42.5cm) deep, but new tubeless screens will soon be available that are shallow and can fit within a bookshelf or be hung directly on the wall. CD players and stereo units now measure 14 inches (35cm) or less in depth. They are designed to be stacked, with all the controls neatly designed on the face of the units; placed on a ready-made bookcase, they can have a sleek built-in look. Trying to fit a bulky record player with a lift-up lid into a standard storage unit may be enough to send one out to buy a compact disc player. The discs take up less space than paperback books, whereas long-playing records, at 12³⁄₈ inches (31cm) square, are difficult to store, since they hang over the edge of standard shelves. When purchasing new entertainment equipment, take your shelf measurements with you to the store and try for as streamlined a look as possible.

Remove the door from a shallow closet and line it with shelves for a built-in look requiring very little effort to achieve. The setbacks on either side of a chimney or fireplace are ideal spots for bookcases and cabinets as in the living room **above**. Here the grandeur of a marble mantelpiece is given the setting it deserves by the addition of bookcases and cabinets surrounded by molding. Because the bookcases are not built flush with the chimney breast, the mantel and the area above it extend still farther into the room. This architectural detail is accented by the bold black-and-white marbleized crown molding that runs around the room. The same warm yellow paint is used on both bookcases and walls so that the addition becomes a part of the original architecture.

ARTWORK ON WALLS

Walls are the natural place for paintings, prints, posters, and any artwork that can be protected by a frame. It is important to consider the framing and arrangement of the artwork in conjunction with the rest of a room's design. The mat and frame, first and foremost, should compliment the work of art. A secondary consideration is the context in which it will hang. Is the room strictly traditional, very modern, or an eclectic mix of styles? An old master's drawing would probably look more at home in a carved wooden frame in a traditional setting, but it could also be striking matted within a thin gilded band on a contemporary wall. The color of the wall behind the work of art will do much to emphasize its color and form. Lighting, too, will draw attention to artwork and contribute to the overall interest of a room.

Several works of art in the same medium and style may be framed the same way, although the size of the frame should be

dictated by the work itself. A large painting or poster on the center of a wall will provide a visual focal point for the whole room. Several pieces hung in a large grouping, like the one **at left**, will achieve the same effect. Here a collection of period interiors rendered in watercolors blankets the wall in a room inspired by the English Regency. The paintings, with colored mats and red accented frames, are all the same size except for three highlighted at the center. This symmetry provides architectural structure to the room.

If a room has interesting architectural details, they can suggest or complement the arrangement of artwork. The paneled walls in the room **above** are typical of the late-nineteenth-century Arts and Craft movement—a period marked by interest in Oriental art—and provide a long horizontal shelf that is perfect for the display of pottery and prints. The single print mounted on one panel is framed with a different-colored mat and becomes part of the arrangement of sculptures and other artifacts on the chest of drawers.

© Phillip H. Ennis

chapter five

FUNCTION AND DESIGN

Windows are one of the most important elements in the functional and aesthetic success of a room's design. They let in natural light; provide a view; keep out rain, cold, insects, and other undesirables; and allow for ventilation of interior space. In office buildings, rooms with windows confer status; we would much rather spend time in a room we can see out of than in a space without windows. The passage of sunlight, entering the east side of a room early in the day and slowly moving around to the south and west as the day goes on, gives us a sense of time passing and keeps us in touch with our daily schedule without having to check a watch or clock. Patches of sunlight falling on the floor or furnishings create a warm and comfortable ambiance, to which any cat will attest. Indirect light from high clerestory windows or skylights brightens a room even on cloudy days. These elements—light, shadow, temperature, and ventilation—all depend on the windows' location, their type and design, and the treatment or covering you choose for them.

ARCHITECTURAL DESIGN

The architectural style of a building is established by the size, shape, and placement of windows on both the exterior and interior. What looks great on the exterior does not always conform to the ideal living arrangement inside and vice versa. Window alterations are common in older homes, and with families shifting their leisure activities from the front porch to the rear deck or terrace, new windows are often installed at the back of the house. This is a happy coincidence, as preservationists around the world stress the importance of protecting historic facades, especially those that face the street. When remodeling or replacing old windows with new ones, however, one should consider carefully the style and architecture of the whole house. Authentic reproductions are readily available in stock sizes or can be made to order; they function as well as contemporary styles and often will not cost much more. A good millworks shop can copy just about any window sash to replace one that is rotten. And in many cases, a rotten sash can be restored. New epoxy compounds, both liquid and paste, are available to strengthen and refill severely deteriorated wood with results as strong as the original. To the first-time homeowner, a peeling or corroded window will look worse than it really is. A good scraping and sanding topped by a good paint job is frequently all that is needed. Before opting for new windows in new sizes and shapes, investigate all the options. A window such as the half-circle Palladian design that has been so popular recently may not age well and will appear more dated in a few years than the simpler double-hung window original to the building.

Window styles run the gamut. Leaded-pane casements, the hinged sashes with diamond-shaped panes from the Middle Ages, are found in Tudor Revival houses. Today these casements are often made of metal and require good paint jobs to prevent corrosion. Wooden casement windows are common in Europe and are paired with sets of solid wood shutters that are used daily, unlike those in North America, which are strictly decorative. Double-hung windows consist of two sashes, one above the other, the glass divided by muntins into panes (often called lights). Because early glass was available only in small sheets, the window sash would contain up to twelve panes depending on the overall size of the sash. As the price of glass decreased and larger sheets were available, the number of panes per sash decreased. In the eighteenth century, twelve over twelve panes and nine over nine panes were common. In the early nineteenth century, it was six over six and later two over two, and in the twentieth century one over one. Today, in an effort to re-create the charm of old, multipaned sashes, manufacturers provide plastic snap-in muntins. Although they make window washing easier, they are flimsy-looking and do little to enhance the design of a house. In registered historic districts, fixed wooden muntins are preferred.

Today, the choices for windows seem endless. Awning windows are hinged along the top of the sash and open out. They are practical in country houses or cabins as they can shed rainwater when open. Jalousie windows have horizontal glass louvers that can also be left partially open during inclement weather. These windows are used most often on porches or in houses in tropical areas. Sliding windows or doors are efficient choices for access to decks or terraces. They are available with multipanes that provide the look of French doors but eliminate the need for space for the door to swing. Real French doors, pairs of multipaned hinged doors, are considered windows because they involve many of the same considerations as windows. Their main advantage is that when open, they provide a wide uninterrupted passage. However, this advantage does pose problems. When it rains, French doors are much more likely to leak, as there is no center "stop" or support to close the doors against. Recently developed French door look-alikes are hinged in the center and open on one side only. They are also weather-stripped to provide a tight seal from wind and water.

EFFECT OF WINDOW TREATMENTS

Windows may be altered visually from the interior by the choice of window treatment. Short windows can be made to look taller, windows in awkward locations can be camouflaged, and windows without a view (those that look out at a concrete wall, for example) can be hung with translucent material so that only the light filters through. To make a window appear taller, use a cornice or valance several inches above the top of the window. The bottom edge of the valance should cover the tops of the curtains and the window frame. To cut a tall window down to size, use an informal treatment of shutters or café curtains across the bottom half only. On windows that have a handsome trim, install curtains or shades inside the reveal, in the space between the trim and the sash of the window. If a window is too plain for the rest of your decorating scheme, cover it up with a dressy treatment.

A window treatment sets the style and mood for an entire room and at the same time offers a wonderful opportunity to create decorative drama. Whether left bare or lavishly festooned in

Courtesy of Gramercy wallpapers and fabrics

Even if your house is not historic, or even old, your choice of furniture might be enhanced by a period window treatment.

As mentioned earlier, color and pattern have a major effect on the style and mood of a room. Heavy, textured fabrics such as velvet or damask in deep, rich colors establish a somber, restful atmosphere. In contrast, sheer fabrics in pale colors invite light into a space, creating a mood that is much more lively. Consider the mood in terms of the use of a room. The somber velvet curtains would be perfect for a study or library, while the sheer curtains would be lovely in a south-facing breakfast nook.

PRACTICAL CONSIDERATIONS

The practical considerations for window treatments include privacy, light control, temperature control, and maintenance. The need for privacy, to prevent outsiders from looking into your home, varies with the type of room and proximity to neighbors. Unless you live in great isolation, bathroom privacy is essential. Another issue that must be considered in the bathroom is moisture; fabrics or other materials used in bathrooms need to be washable, as bleach is the only thorough way to remove mildew. Alternatives are rigid shutters, venetian blinds, or vinyl shades that can be wiped clean with a damp sponge. The need to block the entry of light can be a matter of personal preference. When designing treatments for bedroom windows, remember that while some people depend on the sun to awaken them, others do not want to see the early morning light—a room-darkening window shade installed within the window frame is an inconspicuous and simple solution to this problem. Light control is also important to prevent fading of rugs and upholstery, especially in winter months, when the sun enters a window at a low angle, reaching far into the room.

Temperature control involves the insulating qualities of draperies and shades in colder climates and the need to shield a room from summer sun in hot ones. Exterior awnings and shutters are extremely effective in areas near the equator, where they are

rich fabric, the window will establish the formality or informality and spirit of a space. Period interiors may suggest a window treatment in period style. Museums and house restorations are good sources for ideas; the curators have documents, early-house inventories, and wills that provide information about designs and materials that were popular at various times. Manufacturers who are commissioned to make reproductions of early fabric designs and colors, such as the ones **above** from eighteenth-century Colonial America, for these restorations will often make them available to the general public. Look for fabric collections that are endorsed by well-known historic institutions.

closed during the heat of midday and later opened to admit cool evening breezes. Although many people are reliant on mechanical air conditioning, far simpler cooling methods can work and reduce reliance on electricity.

Kitchen windows require careful considerations for safety reasons. A classic warning is to avoid flowing curtains near the open flame of a cooktop. Window treatments that are easy to wash or wipe clean are a must in cooking areas, where fatty oils and grease can float through the air and land on walls and windows alike.

CHOOSING AND COMBINING FABRICS, COLORS, AND PATTERNS

Window dressing involves many choices. Are you going to use a shade or blind? Will you have curtains or drapery? Is a valance or cornice necessary or desirable? If you have long drapery, will you need an undercurtain of lace or a sheer fabric for added privacy in the daytime? Since every window is different, with a different set of problems and requirements, it is hard to make general rules for what fabric or material to use. But by answering a number of simple questions, some that are practical and some that deal with taste, you can whittle down the vast array of choices until you have a handsome, workable window treatment. Certain rooms suggest certain types of fabrics. There are many infant and juvenile patterns designed just for children's bedrooms. Some adults may feel that their bedroom should be restful, while others may crave color and pattern to lift their spirits. There are also differences in thinking between some men and women. But the old adage that floral "feminine" designs are just for women and dark solid colors or stripes are masculine just doesn't work anymore in our shared lives. That was fine when women had their own boudoirs and dressing areas and men slept and dressed in wood-paneled splendor

across the hall. Today men and women are more likely to decide on a look that complements their home, their interests, and their lifestyle.

There are millions of designs and an enormous number of fabric types from which to choose. You can start with the choice of a type of fabric. Consider these common fabrics, which range from light to heavy weight: sheer polyester, cotton voile and organdy, cotton and polyester lace, silk, broadcloth, chintz or polished cotton, cotton sateen, sailcloth or duck, twill, cotton, linen or wool damask, brocade, tapestry, cotton velveteen, cotton or silk velvet. All of these fabrics are available in colors and with printed patterns in large, medium, and small scales. Woven patterns in cotton or blends include stripes, checks, and plaids.

Throughout this book you can see window treatments that have been chosen to coordinate with the other fabrics, colors, and patterns in the same rooms. To better understand why these combinations are successful, we can break down the schemes to identify their unifying elements. For instance, in the living room on page 116, dark walls are the foil for three distinctive patterns: a bold chintz on the sofa and at the windows, a striped chair in the foreground, and a small overall pattern for the carpet. The colors red, green, and white, repeated in these patterns, tie them all together. Another example can be seen in the formal sitting room on the left of page 128, in which the main attraction is a golden harp. The color scheme of yellow, blue, and white with leafy green is established in the large-patterned chintz drapery and is repeated in the smaller pattern on the chair and ottoman and the medium-scaled pattern of the rug. This combination of large, medium, and small patterns conforms to the flexible rule of choosing three patterns in three scales. Wonderful details such as the brilliant yellow of the wall and the ruffled edging on the drapery give the room extra spark. For a dramatic mixing of patterns and colors, consider the elegant living room on page 118, which combines dark walls with bold floral chintz curtains. The reds, golds, greens, and tans of the chintz suggested the other fabrics: the woven green

© Eric Roth, linens by Malibar Grove

stripe on the chair, the gold velvet on the bench, the deep red of the rug, and even the leopard fabric in the foreground. Again the scales of the patterns are large, medium, and small.

Remember that elements other than textiles, such as the books on a shelf, contribute pattern and color. In the library on page 120, plain drapery has a greater effect than a busy window treatment would have had. The broad expanse of off-white linen is contrasted by the dark paneled walls. The play of pattern here ranges from the medium-sized flowers on the ottoman, to smaller flowers in the rug and throw pillows, to the plaid of the

chair and the array of book bindings on the shelves. Another eclectic room is found in the kitchen on the left of page 100. In this room, textures are added to pattern in a combination of painted wood wainscoting, ceramic tile, oak furniture, and colorful fabrics.

As you can see, pattern and texture can present themselves in unusual and unexpected ways. A more tailored look is achieved in the small apartment on the right of page 128, where solid colors on the walls and large upholstered pieces are combined with geometric patterns in three scales: large windowpane-check shades, shutter louvers, and the small overall pattern of the rug. The colors may be neutral, black, brown, and white, but they are just as important to the overall look. The room on the right of page 129 provides one final example of a successful mixture of patterns. This room is styled in a takeoff of the most cluttered of all design periods, the Edwardian age at the end of the Victorian era in England. Striped window shades and wall coverings are combined with a large floral on the sofa and a very complex Oriental rug. The furniture is a mix of formal carving and gilding with exotica from all over the world. However, the mixture of fabric patterns and colors with the different furniture finishes results in a very composed and comfortable scheme.

To make your window-design process easier, here is a chain of events to follow. From your clipping file establish the mood and style—dark or light walls, dark or light window treatment—and the type of treatment—drapery or shades, long or short. Then go out and look for fabrics close to the color and pattern you have in mind. Bring samples home and decide on the final choice for the room. If you are planning to change the wall color or covering, review paint, paper, and fabric samples together. Once the wall color or covering and the main fabric for the windows are chosen, you can refine the scheme. Add the type of hardware, the heading, lining material, trimming, and tiebacks. Experienced shoppers and professionals may be able to gather all the elements in one trip, but don't be surprised if your idea changes a bit in the process and you have to go out again.

SPECIAL WINDOWS

Some windows are so attractive that the best treatment is to leave them bare, highlighting their architectural detail. Of course, privacy and light control may have to be taken into account, but if the room faces a private garden and you don't mind the dawn's light, the beauty of the window will far surpass these practical considerations. Wonderful window artifacts are found in old buildings rehabilitated for modern apartment use. If you can afford it, fine craftspeople who can re-create period windows or make strikingly modern new ones can be found in many communities. Making the most of these architectural assets can be the key to your decorating scheme.

Rooms on top floors often have dormer windows that poke out from the roof, and basement-level rooms often look out on gardens at eye level. The bedroom tucked in at the top of the house **on page 109** has a bird's-eye view of the garden beyond. The elliptical window with its delicate lead tracery is a prominent feature of the Adam style in late-eighteenth-century England and the Federal period in North America. The ivory color scheme showcases the furnishings of a later date, which add a subtle element of whimsy to the decorative scheme.

© Balthazar Korab

floor and lots of windows to let in the daylight, may have been a conservatory, a room designed for rare tropical plants.

Putting an addition on an older home need not require the elimination of wonderful old windows that are in the common wall; they can be left to look out on a new hallway or converted to another use, like the window in the beautiful old parlor **below**, which has been closed up on one side with artificial lighting installed at the rear. The light source is masked by the etched glass panes, and shelves hold a collection of blue and lavender antique glass. The window now provides soft lighting in a somber room, and the glassware glows in jewellike colors.

Houses of many periods have unique windows: Queen Anne–style houses from the late Victorian era are blessed with oval, diamond-shaped, or rectangular windows with stained glass; and the Gothic Revival in the mid-1800s reintroduced windows with pointed arches and oriels, large bay windows that project from the side of the building. In the very grand early twentieth-century house **at left**, leaded glass windows line an alcove that is separated from the main room by Greek columns and trim. In an allusion to the sweeping drapery in classical art, the doorway is swagged and draped with English country chintz, a touch that brings this room down to earth. A simpler treatment of an equally grand residence can be seen **above**, where shirred curtains screen the lower sash below textured stained glass windows. Slim rods at the top and bottom hold the curtains in place. A century ago this room, with a practical tile

DRAPERY

Drapery is the formal dress for windows that reside in elegant, stylized settings. The demeanor of windows dressed with drapery is tall, graceful, and rather staid. They are unruffled by breezes, and movement, if any, is languid and quiet. The fabrics are quite heavy, lined with cotton sateen, and sometimes interlined. When a lighter fabric such as chintz or polished cotton is chosen for formal drapery, it is interlined with white cotton flannel to give it body and ensure full, rounded folds. Other fabrics that are rich in color and pattern and of the appropriate weight are damasks, silks, brocades, velvets, linens, and tapestry weaves. Lining fabrics are traditionally white or off-white and are intended to provide a uniform look from the exterior of the house. When intentionally allowing the lining to show through the face fabric, stronger lining colors may be used. Heavy linings are designed to block out light and to insulate, cutting down on heat loss through window glass.

There are many headings for drapery, the most common being pinch pleats. Variations are box pleats, which are wider and therefore more square in shape, cartridge and pencil pleats, very slender pleats about the size of a pencil. Drapery may hang straight or be pulled back to the window frame on each side with a tieback, a rosette, or a metal or wood hold-back. Standard hem lengths reach the sill, the bottom of the apron (the trim below the sill), or the floor; in very luxurious rooms, the drapery can be an extra 4 to 6 inches (10 to 15cm) long and the excess fabric "puddled" on the floor.

Drapery Hardware

Since drapery is the heaviest window treatment, a traverse rod is usually necessary to enable it to be opened and closed. The traverse rod consists of metal loops or carriers connected to cords that are operated from one side of the window. Traverse rods can be two-way draw, opening at the center, or one-way draw, opening from either side. Double traverse are available for two layers of draperies, for a heavier set on the room side and a lighter set of sheer, glass, or casement curtains next to the window. They also come as a combination of traverse rod plus a plain curtain rod next to the window, or with a valance rod in front of the traverse rod. Traverse rods come in different shapes for different situations: bay windows, corner windows, or bow windows. Most rods can be custom-fit to your particular window. Decorative traverse rods function in the same manner as conventional ones except that they are meant to show above the curtain heading. What looks like a decorative pole with rings really hides a traverse mechanism whose half-circle rings show on the front. Special brackets for the decorative pole also support a stationary curtain rod for casement curtains behind the decorative pole.

Window style and the type of hardware you plan to use are the determining factors when deciding on the length of a traverse rod and the height at which to install it. When hanging a drapery with a shirred or pleated heading, it is best to place the rod at least 4 inches (10cm) above the window glass so that the back of the rod and the heading will not show from the outside of the window. A traverse rod must be wide enough to accommodate the stackback, the drapery width when the treatment is completely opened and stacked at each side. As a general rule, add about one third of the actual window glass width to each side of the window for windows up to 60 inches (150cm) wide, one fourth of the glass width for windows up to 80 inches (200cm) wide, and one fifth of the glass width for larger windows. For instance, if the glass area is 36 inches (90cm) wide, the window will need a stackback allowance of 12 inches (30cm) on each side. Therefore, the length of the rod is determined by adding 36 inches (90cm) for the glass plus 24 inches (60cm) for the stackback, equaling a rod length of 60 inches (150cm). If the rod is long, it may require one or two extra support brackets. Brackets and extenders of various lengths are available to enable the drapery to clear the window trim and hang unobstructed to the sill, apron, or floor.

VALANCES

A valance, or cornice, is the fabric or structural covering that hides the heading and hardware at the top of window drapery. Cornices are wooden boxes with molding that become part of the architecture of the room and can be painted or upholstered with padding and fabric. Traditional fabric-covered cornices are shaped along the bottom edges in geometric steps or in flow-

ing curves and curlicues, like the upholstered ones topping the draperies of gray-blue damask in the French music room **above**. The bottom edges of the cornices are finished with matching cording that follows the curves. Light reflected from the warm apricot walls bathes the Louis XV–style furniture in a golden glow.

Fabric valances are softer, with pleated or gathered headings. A heading with several rows of gathers much like smocking on a child's dress is called ruching. In the child's room **at upper right**, the same effect is achieved with valances with pencil pleated headings and a narrowly striped fabric. The combination of slim pleats with a double ruffled edge has the charm of a little girl's party dress. The fullness or amount of fabric used is important in a pleated or gathered valance; unless the valance is designed as a flat panel, fabric that is three or even four times the width of the window is needed to avoid a skimpy look. Contrasting trim on the valance, curtains, and pillow shams draws attention and is an effective finishing touch.

In a departure from the more formal treatments, the valance in the bedroom **at lower left** is based on swags but is made of lightweight white fabric that is connected by puffy knots at the intersections. White window shades for privacy are hidden behind the swags and can be drawn at night. The same classic swags also soften the lines of the metal-framed bed and end in graceful drapery at each corner.

Valances and cornices can be used without drapery or curtains; they are also useful over roller shades and various types of blinds.

SWAGS AND JABOTS

Swags and jabots are, respectively, the horizontal drape of fabric across the top of a window and the pair of vertical panels, sometimes called waterfalls, at each side. In some cases, they are used as valances over long drapery; in others they grace a plain window or are paired with shutters, shades, or blinds. The edges of the swag are cut on the diagonal, and it is difficult to match the lining and face fabrics at the seams. For this reason, a ruffle or fringe is often stitched into the seam along the edges. Since the lining shows along the edge of the swag and in the folds of the jabot, a contrasting fabric is often used. For a tailored effect, solids can be lined with contrasting colors, as in the classic red-and-gold example in the nineteenth-century dining room **on the left of page 116**. The double swag reveals a center swag of the same gold fabric that lines the jabots at each side. A deep fringe adorns the swags and a narrower braid accents the jabots. Casement or under-curtains of thin cotton lawn are held back by rosettes and left to hang freely for privacy. Since the woodwork around the window is so handsome, this treatment was designed to fit within the window trim.

A softer feeling is achieved when floral fabrics are combined with fine stripes, plaids, or checks. In the large living room **on the right of page 116**, a swag and jabot in giant scale function as a valance over drapery and sheer undercurtains. Dark green

are bold and almost chubby and seem to bring the windows down to earth. Solid yellow scallops and a fringed braid outline the edges, a wonderful finishing touch in this charming room.

Be aware that the color or pattern of the lining of the swag and jabot might show through the top fabric when lit from behind, so check to be sure the effect is pleasing. If not, use an interlining in between. Although the swag and jabot appear to be one piece draped over a wooden pole, they are usually made separately and attached to the pole in a way that allows the folds to hang properly. A thin, lightweight, reversible fabric can be looped over a pole and arranged to fall in a more natural manner.

trim inserted in the seam smooths the transition between the floral chintz and plaid lining. To balance the large-scale pattern in the room, the same chintz is also used on the sofa.

Softness can also come from the way the fabric is arranged. The rather regal bedroom **on the left of page 117** is given a country look with lots of cottage-style chintz at the windows. Here the jabots are gathered at the top, and the edges ruffle gently rather than fall into neatly turned pleats. These swags and jabots

Hardware for Swags and Jabots

Swags or festoons with jabots can be hung from a curtain pole or mounted on a box or board valance. The pole itself can be very decorative, designed to coordinate with the fabrics or woodwork in the room. Classic designs have fluted poles with turned finials at each end. Base-metal poles can be finished to look like brass, wrought iron, pewter, silver, or copper. Wooden poles with fancy painted finishes often pick up the colors of the window fabrics. Sculptured finials range from simple urn shapes to hand-carved flowers, animals, birds, and insects. Rosettes are also used to support swag and jabot treatments, usually when the fabric is lightweight and reversible and can be naturally draped or wrapped around the rosette and allowed to fall down each side of the window. Rosettes come in metal with brass, gold, silver, or pewter finishes and in painted wood or synthetic compositions. Antique rosettes can be found in pressed glass in milky white or brilliant colors.

The swag and jabot is a formal design, but made up in simple fabrics, it can provide a sophisticated fillip to a country interior. In a twist, the tiny dining nook **at right** combines a bamboo pole and inexpensive bamboo blinds with two lengths of cotton print. The fabric is stitched together down each edge so it becomes reversible and is simply draped over the pole—no hooks, pins, or tacks—and it can be easily removed for laundering and then put back up. The same fabric covers the lampshade and the lamp cord hung from the ceiling. A plywood circle on hardware-store legs has been transformed into a draped table with orange skirt and plaid topper; a rattan bistro chair completes the setting. The result is a cheery breakfast nook created without strain on the budget.

117

CURTAINS

A curtain hung from a rigid pole is among the earliest known window treatments. The interest of the ancient Greeks in beautiful flowing folds of fabric is most evident in their sculpture, and it takes only a small leap of faith to imagine colorful drapery in their homes as well. Byzantine mosaics from fifth-century Italy depict patterned curtains with fringed hems hung from white poles. Medieval bed hangings were suspended in the same way. Today curtain poles are made from wrought iron, copper, brass, synthetic materials, and wood that is either left plain or carved and fluted with decorative finials added to the ends. Some poles incorporate traverse rod mechanisms. The fabric panels are hung from fabric loops or wooden or metal rings, which are sewn or pinned to the top edge. The curtain headings are often pleated and attached to the curtain rings at the tops of the pleats. The pole can be treated as part of the woodwork or architecture, considered metal hardware along with doorknobs and cabinet pulls, or covered with fabric as a decorative element of the window treatment.

The curtain and pole treatment can be extremely formal, very simple, or even rustic—coarse muslin could be hung from a bark-covered twig. The materials used and the way they are assembled and integrated with the rest of the furnishings do much to set the mood of a room. In the grand library **at far left**, the black lacquered poles with gilded highlights match the walls and pay subtle respect to the magnificent gilt patterns on the japanned secretary. More yellow-gold glitters from the brass rings and the flood of sunlight coming through the yellow balloon shades hung behind the curtains. The progression from dark tones to the light at the windows is unusual and instructive. The scheme evolves from brown-black walls and black-lacquer and dark-wood furniture to medium-toned books and rug, to lighter upholstery on the chair and bench, and finally to the cream-colored chintz and pale shades that warm and brighten the daylight.

In the room **on the left of page 120**, the look is relaxed but still dressy. Black rings on a wrought-iron pole provide support for champagne-colored curtains with gathered headings. The plaid shade underneath is installed at the same level as the pole for a crisp, uniform look and is easily raised and lowered behind the stationary curtains.

A curtain design does not have to be complicated to make a strong statement. The freshly starched look of white curtain poles, white trim, pearly pale walls, and full-bodied gray linen is a striking setting for the furnishings in the classical mode located

at top right. The extra-long curtains emphasize the height of the room; the pair on the right are hung above the window to make it appear as tall as the doors. A point of interest is that the ceiling, above the white crown molding, is painted the same color as the walls. Everything is clean and stately here, creating a formality very different from that of the library on page 118.

The proportion of the fabric to window width can vary greatly. In general, thinner fabrics are given more fullness so as not to seem skimpy, while heavier ones are given less so as not to appear crowded. If a very tailored effect is desired, a curtain might have no softness at all. In the library/sitting room **at bottom right**, a flat curtain with buttoned tabs piped in crimson is hung so that the fabric falls into shallow folds with a distinctly architectural look. The whimsical window treatment **on page 121**, which eliminates the curtain pole altogether and can be tacked up in minutes, has the same effect. Unlined cotton is

gathered in soft pleats and stapled to the inside of the window frame. Alternating red and yellow bows were then tacked to the top of each pleat. The fabric panels are swept back and draped over brass rosettes at the edges of the trim. Classical references in this room are right up-to-date combined with Navaho-like weavings in campy shades of yellow, red, and purple.

SHEER CURTAINS

Curtains made from sheer or translucent, see-through fabrics are not lined and are, therefore, simple in design and construction. The more diaphanous sheers are soft and easy to drape and can be shirred (gathered) into tight folds. Embroidered sheers and laces are a bit stiffer and are gathered more loosely to better display their pattern. In the past, sheer curtains were considered the summer treatment. Our grandmothers and great-grandmothers took down their heavy drapery for cleaning in the spring and did not put it back up until autumn. The casement curtains, the sheer undercurtains closest to the window sash, were washed, starched, and put up again. They were pale in color and light enough to waft in the summer's breeze, ideal for the hot months before the age of air-conditioning. At the same time, the summer slipcovers in muslin, cotton ticking, or light-colored prints were put on the furniture, and the whole house looked cool and refreshing. This light and airy feeling is most popular today. The current revival of classical designs in furniture and fabrics has created renewed interest in the styles of Napoleon's France, when Josephine and the ladies of her court dressed in thin, printed cottons that flowed from Empire waistlines down to the floor. Curtains of this period took on the same appearance: sheer festoons trimmed with tassel fringe, all in white or very small patterns. This look is sophisticated enough for city residences as well as country houses, where it adds a little formality with a lighthearted touch.

Lace sheers are an appropriate way to add light to traditionally dark Victorian interiors. In the sitting room **on the left on**

this page, very simple lace curtains are shirred or gathered on rods set within the dark oak window frames. The lace has the same translucent effect as the leaded-glass window above it and complements the window without overwheleming it.

In the bedroom **at right**, the center window, located between a second window (not shown) and the porch door, is extended to the ceiling with a flexible rod shaped in an arch to fit the space. The sheer fabric is gathered across the top and tied back at each side. The door on the left and a window on the right are draped to the floor for additional privacy. The floral wallpaper is a charming choice with the Victorian bed, lighting, and patchwork quilt.

Sheers filter light rather than blocking it, so if true privacy is desired, they must be used in conjunction with shades or shutters. When privacy is not the issue, they are an ideal finish to a naked window, adding softness and pattern and making you feel less exposed without hemming you in. **On page 123**, lacy

curtains add a light and cooling touch to a bright country kitchen. Gently swagged, they function as deep valances and allow direct sun on the plant stand below. Without competition, the simple wallpaper has a crisp assertiveness.

CAFE AND SASH CURTAINS

Café curtains have come a long way from the boulevards of Paris that made them famous. In cafés, these curtains ran across the bottom half of the window and were hung on rods with small rings that made it easy to slide them open or closed. Now found everywhere, this basic curtain can solve a myriad of problems, providing privacy while allowing a view and the passage of light. Two or even three tiers of café curtains will cover a

© Jessie Walker Associates

© Phillip H. Ennis

tall window or door. A shallow curtain at the top of the window often serves as a valance over a standard café curtain running across the bottom half. The fabrics used are usually informal printed cottons of stripes, checks, and plaids. They can be lined to present a finished look to the street or yard.

Café curtains can also have gathered, ruched, scalloped, or pleated headings. They can be sewn with casings at the top, like those gathered on spring tension rods in the kitchen window **above**. The soft rose color of the windowpane check complements the rose of the displayed English pottery. Set within the

© Phillip H. Ennis

Sash curtains are a refinement of café curtains. They are used on windows and doors where a loose, flowing curtain would get in the way. The sash curtain is shirred (gathered) onto a top and bottom rod and slightly stretched between the rods to hold it taut. Silk organza and fine lace are used for sash curtains in formal settings, for the interiors of china cabinets or secretary doors, and for interior French doors between, for instance, a foyer and a dining room. Kitchen cabinets with glass doors can become a decorative asset when lined with a bright cotton print, a boon for those who like the look of glass-paned doors but want to hide the cereal boxes.

Café and Sash Curtain Hardware

Hardware for café curtains is readily available. Half-inch (13mm) brass rods with finials and small brass rings are basic and good-looking. Some curtain companies sell wooden brackets to hold wooden dowel rods for a country or informal room. These rods can be painted to match the window trim or to coordinate with the curtains. A woodworker handy with a jigsaw can easily make custom brackets in any size or shape from half-inch (13mm) stock. Also available for café curtains are spring tension rods that have rubber tips and can be adjusted to fit within the window frame. They do not need brackets and are easy to install or move. Metal or plastic curtain rings come in brass or white. Wood rings can also be painted to match. Tabs or loops of fabric, woven tape, or ribbon sewn to the curtain are an alternative to curtain rings.

Very slim metal rods with small metal brackets are sold for sash curtains. The rods must be carefully positioned to create enough tension to hold the curtain taut without causing the rod to bow. The rods for larger curtains, such as those on a French door, are rectangular in profile and wider so they will not bend under tension. The brackets are affixed to the surface of the door or window sash. Since many sash curtains are sheer or white, these rods are usually available in a white finish.

reveal of the nicely trimmed window and hemmed at the sill, these curtains will not interfere with the countertop area.

Cotton lace curtains in bold provincial patterns are seen in the windows of old stone houses throughout Europe. The look is charming and practical, as the lace can be washed, hung to dry, and put back up. While some avid needleworkers still choose to crochet their own curtains, today there are many ready-made patterns available, often with motifs to fit the use of the room. The coffeepot-trimmed pair **above** brings this old city kitchen up to date without a great deal of construction or expense; there is an eyelet pattern, called beading, worked at the top that slides easily over the curtain rod. Lots of white paint on furniture, trim, and cabinets brightens what was a dark, dingy space. The wallpaper with border provides some color but maintains the light, bright feeling.

125

SHADES, BLINDS, AND SHUTTERS

Today shades, blinds, and shutters can solve a multitude of problems without sacrificing glamour or luxury. Interior shutters of gleaming mahogany block out the fading rays of sun and noise from the street. Blinds now run the gamut from traditional wooden venetians to transparent plastic louvers that work like sunglasses. Shades can be the flat roller variety, as simple as plain cloth, or an elaborate construction of gathers and puffs. To make your planning easier, fabric shades, the ones made with decorative fabrics, are discussed first. The latter half of the chapter includes shades, blinds, and shutters that offer a more architectural effect: the verticals, venetians, and the new synthetic honeycomb shades.

FABRIC SHADES

A fabric shade by any name—Austrian, balloon, Roman, or accordion—can solve a number of window problems with zip or grace, depending on your style and mood. They can be full-blown, blousey affairs, using yards of sumptuous fabric, or neat, efficient models that stay within the window's trim. Windows with radiators, air conditioners, or deep ledges for windowsills are dif-ficult to treat with floor-length drapery; even if the draperies can reach the floor on each side of the window they may not close across the center. A shade installed behind the drapery is the perfect solution, fulfilling the need to control light, heat, and cold and providing privacy in a decorative and practical manner. Unlined shades in washable fabrics are good choices for windows above a kitchen counter. Shades with blackout lining are great for bedrooms. Insulating linings will cut drafts and prevent heat loss in winter and reflect the sun's heat in summer. All of these types of shades operate with cords and pulleys on the rear, which are attached to a narrow board at the top of the window and secured by a cleat on the trim.

Austrian shades feature vertical rows of stitched gathers spaced at intervals down the length; they are often made in sheer fabrics and used behind long drapery. The shade pulls up along the gathered lines, puffing the hem into a scallop. The bottom edge is frequently trimmed with fringe. **On the left of page 128**, sheer Austrian shades form the backdrop of a purely romantic setting. Bow windows such as these pose special problems because of the continuous curve. Here, a flexible rod bent to fit holds the top of the shade in place, while the operat-

© Philip H. Ennis

construction, and the setting. Those **on page 126**, made of a peach-and-green striped silk, have gathered headings and ruffled hems and are dressy enough for a formal city apartment. At night they are lowered to the ledge behind the sofa and form a handsome background for the room's floral furnishings.

A completely different interpretation can be seen in the apartment living room **below**. Here, tailored balloon shades with inverted pleats at the top are given special emphasis by cornices of crown molding. The colors of the plaid are continued in stripes across the molding, while louvered shutters at the bottom of the window provide privacy, light, and ventilation. **At right**, a relaxed variation of the balloon shade is shown, casting a warm glow over a monochromatic sitting room.

The Roman shade has no fullness across its width; because of the special tapes carrying the cords on the back, the fabric creases into neat horizontal folds as it is raised. If the shade is

© Bill Rothschild, Design: Denise Balassi

ing cords run behind it. The festooned valance and curtains trimmed with pleated yellow chintz hang from a blue-painted pole, in bright contrast with the yellow walls.

The balloon shade is similar to the Austrian shade, but the fabric gathers up only when the shade is raised, falling in a row of scallops across the bottom. Vertical stripes are especially well suited to balloon shades, as they drape into interesting patterns when the shade is pulled up. Balloon shades can be formal or informal, depending upon the fabric used, the particulars of the

BLINDS AND SHUTTERS

Blinds and shutters can be considered architectural elements in a room's design. That is not to deny their decorative effect, but to emphasize their mechanical function and the role they play in the structure of a space, rather than in its dressing. Shutters, made of wood and part of the window trim, are obviously architectural. Less obvious are the various types of blinds developed to cover the large expanses of glass in modern twentieth-century buildings. Often these blinds are specified by the architect to ensure that all the windows have a uniform look on the exterior as well as the interior. In contemporary design, a window may be the equivalent of an entire wall, so

cut with extra length, additional folds can be tacked permanently in place on the face so that it appears pleated even when it is down. The Roman shades **at right** have a crisp, military air, and combined with the narrow stripe on the walls, they lend order to this small apartment furnished with opulent Victoriana. When there is enough depth to the reveal, the shade can be installed inside the frame, as it is here, a good idea in close quarters or where the trim is too nice to hide.

Accordion shades have folds of only 1 to 4 inches (2.5 to 10cm) deep. They are made of stiffened fabric with holes punched in rows down the length; the sash cords are passed in and out of the holes, and the shade resembles a closed fan when pulled all the way up. Accordion shades can be custom made from drapery and curtain fabric by workshops specializing in window treatments. Mass-produced accordion shades are also available in many fabrics and colors.

the appearance of whatever covers it will be very important. Shutters and blinds fulfill the same needs as other window treatments, but they do so in geometric planes with linear accents rather than flowing folds of curtains and drapery; large expanses of shutters and blinds can give a room a hard, crisp finish.

Classic venetian blinds, made from wood and painted or stained in wood tones, have been in use for hundreds of years. The tapes on venetian blinds can be decorative, made of cotton twill in solid colors or woven stripes, or embroidered in patterns like ribbon. Today wood venetians are available with 1- and 2-inch (2.5- and 50cm) wide vanes. For many years wide-vaned metal venetians were ubiquitous, and they are often the first to go in a renovation, except in rooms where 1950s fabrics and furniture reign. In these rooms, off-white, clunky blinds tap with a familiar nostalgic ping as they are buffeted by the wind. Mini-blinds are miniature versions of venetian blinds, offered with 1/2-inch (13mm) and 1-inch (2.5cm) wide metal vanes in hundreds of colors and metal finishes. Gold, silver, and bronze mini-blinds provide a sophisticated sheen to the most upscale interiors. Some plastic-vaned mini-venetians are transparent and function like dark glasses.

Vertical blinds are another architectural asset. Very practical, they can be drawn across the window like a drapery, while the individual vertical vanes are adjustable to control light and temperature. Vertical blinds are available in the same types of material as roller shades—opaque and translucent—in a variety of colors and textures. In the starkly contemporary setting **at left**, vertical blinds control the sun and provide subtle architectural interest. The few accessories, including the cow-skin rug, blue and peach throw pillows, two red roses each placed in a bud vase, and a flowering plant, stand out against the neutral furnishings and floor.

Matchstick and bamboo blinds are made of thin strips of wood and roll up with cords and pulleys. They are inexpensive and informal treatments, whether in their natural finish or painted to coordinate with the room. Combination matchstick and fiber-woven blinds have a handcrafted, homespun look.

Interior wooden shutters also fall into the architectural category. They are available in a variety of sizes. Multifold, with fixed or adjustable louvers, shutters can be installed in pairs like exterior shutters across part of the window or in tiers. Stained or painted, they are flexible, practical, and good-looking, giving a softer finish to a room than vertical blinds do. The adjustable-louvered shutters **on page 132** screen a large plate-glass window in a small study. Painted a cream color, the shutters act as a pleasantly textured backdrop to the contemporary furnishings and allow for soft, filtered natural light. When folded back on each side, they take up a minimum of space and create an attractive frame for the window opening.

Roller shades, although overshadowed by mini-blinds in recent years, are still an inexpensive standby. Used alone or under drapery or curtain treatments, roller shades provide privacy and control light. They are also insulating, preventing heat from radiating out of a room through the window glass. Shade cloths range from old-fashioned dark green blackouts (used in homes during World War II) to translucent textures in all colors and a small variety of patterns. Roller shades can be laminated with fabric and are sold in kits with instructions.

The newest mass-produced shades and blinds offer function and flexibility in a variety of looks. Translucent fabric shades inspired by venetian blinds consist of two panels of fabric linked by vanelike strips of fabric stitched in between. This shade can be raised, lowered, and adjusted so that the vanes are horizontal (the open position) or vertical to further control the light. When pulled up to the top of the window, the fabric is compressed and completely hidden by a head rail. This shade is soft-looking, filtering the light like a sheer or lace curtain.

Honeycomb shades are another modern innovation. These window treatments consist of two layers of pleated material fused together along the creases to form tubes. Since the tubes create pockets of dead air, these shades insulate the window

from hot sun and exterior cold. The shades can be installed from a simple header to hang free like a conventional venetian blind, or they can be installed with a track on each side of the window opening and raised from the bottom up, the top down, or both ways at the same time. Since the tracks are flexible, these shades can be installed in odd-shaped windows, skylights, clerestory windows (installed high on the wall), and curved window walls such as in greenhouses. With a long-handled pole, the shades on hard-to-reach windows can still be opened and closed. The flexible track can even be installed in a half-circle, Palladian window, with the honeycomb shade opening and closing like a pleated fan.

As an option for covering sliding glass doors or large windows, honeycomb shades are also available with the pleats running vertically. These have a track, with operating cords along the top, but the bottom edge hangs free. Even with very wide windows or doors, the stacking area at the side amounts to only 6 to 8 inches (15 to 20cm) when the shade is open. Honeycomb shades come in a variety of fabrics, colors, and patterns with matching or contrasting fabrics on the face and back. The material can be sheer, semitransparent, translucent, or opaque, and one shade can be made up of two fabrics, one for the top section of the shade and one for the bottom section. If the bottom part is opaque, the shade can be adjusted so that the whole window is covered with the opaque section, completely blocking light for sleeping. Or the shade can be adjusted so that a translucent section covers the window to let in daylight while still providing privacy. A lightweight metal bar separates the two sections and is raised or lowered depending on the desired position. A third option is to raise the whole shade until it is hidden within the header, leaving the window bare.

The pleats on honeycomb shades come in three sizes: 3/8 inch (9mm), 3/4 inch (19mm), and 2 inches (5cm), depending on the

fabric choice. A triple honeycomb shade with three layers of tubes has been designed for extra energy efficiency, with an R-value (the resistance of heat flow) up to 5.6, and would make a big difference in heating and cooling costs in extreme climates. In winter, most of the heat loss from a building is radiated away through the window glass. Many honeycomb shades can have a different face and backing fabric, so that all the windows look the same from the exterior but differ from room to room on the interior.

Large expanses of shade, whether honeycombs, verticle blinds, or roller shades, can be operated by motor when they are too heavy or awkward to open and close by hand. The motors can be controlled by switch or remote control and can be connected to temperature-sensitive thermostats to raise or lower the shades according to changes in interior temperature. First developed for commercial greenhouses to protect the plants from frost or overheating, these systems also work well in large buildings or in houses where energy costs and comfort would benefit from constant temperature control. Even in moderate climates, modern houses with skylights and many large windows can become extremely hot on sunny days and chilly in winter without some sort of insulating shade.

Although in a different category and not truly a decorative window treatment, the problem of heat gain and loss can also be controlled by using insulating glass or by adding sun-control films directly to the glass. The latter can be especially helpful in preventing fading and deterioration to rugs, carpet, and upholstery fabrics. Valuable Oriental rugs are particularly vulnerable to the destructiveness of the sun.

A window treatment will enhance the function of your home, making it more comfortable and secure, and will be a vital part of the design of your personal environment. Enjoy the creative process involved in picking out the window treatment that is best for you and take time to savor the results.

p a r t   t h r e e

BATHROOMS

STYLE AND MOOD

A bathroom. Every dwelling has at least one. It takes only a moment's thought to recognize that the bathroom is one of the most important rooms in your home: it has to work, it takes abuse from steam or water, it is probably used by more than one person, and it may do double duty as a laundry, linen closet, or dressing area. In fact, there is a good chance that the bath will need refurbishing, if not renovation, more often than any other room in the house.

Because the bathroom is so vital and so prone to wear, its design should be given more than just passing thought. Whether you are building a new house, renovating an old one, or simply planning a face-lift for an existing bath, you want to end up with a room that functions well and looks wonderful.

Before you plan the specifics of a new bathroom, you should have an idea of the style and the mood you want to establish. Think of style in terms of architecture: period or modern, ornate or sleek. Think of mood in terms of ambience: utilitarian or luxurious, formal or casual, clinical or cozy. The overall style of your home will no doubt influence the choices you make, but because the bathroom receives so much use and is usually so self-contained, you may wish to make a stylistic departure in it.

The mood and style you choose will determine the look of your bathroom. The Old World ambience of the room **at left** takes its cue from the elegant, deep-set window with significant moldings and the half-tiled walls with bull-nose trim. With the fixtures, tile, and trim all in white, your eye is drawn at once to the hand-painted vistas of the mural, which also serve to expand the narrow room. Note the complementary use of white and chrome fittings, with the contrast of wood tones and green for accent. This is, of course, a very special room, at once formal and serene.

STYLE

As you think about the look you want for your bath, consider the architectural style. Is the house old, or a reproduction of a particular period? Colonial or Early American, or one of the various revivals of those styles? Victorian? Arts and Crafts? Art Deco? Is it of a particular regional style? Is it a very modern house, or perhaps a loft in a converted commercial space? Is the house of a style that predates indoor plumbing, and if so, how do you wish to integrate the bath with the rest of the home?

137

Think about the proportions. Are the rooms spacious or tiny, the windows large or small? Is the interior trim generous or minimal, ornate and richly molded or simple? If you are redoing rather than building new, do you like what you see? Are you able to change the size of the room by adding on or borrowing from a neighboring space? You may not be able to do this, but it is very often possible to change the fenestration, increasing the natural light and air and making the room seem more spacious. Or perhaps you can't bear the old aluminum-framed awning window and want to replace it with multilight wooden sash. Sometimes an existing ceiling can be raised or removed, exposing beams that add character as well as height. Conversely, if the room is cavernous, perhaps dropping the ceiling or raising the floor in some or all of it will make it more comfortable.

If no major architectural changes are in order, is the trim satisfactory? If you are planning a complete redo, you will have to retrim the room. But even if this is not necessary, you may wish to do it anyhow. Moldings enhance and can even create architectural character, so consider choosing a new profile or beefing up the proportions of door, window, and baseboard trim, or think about adding wainscoting, a chair rail, or crown molding. Let your thoughts about architectural style percolate while you think about cabinetry; if the cabinets are not of a piece with the trim, they should be complementary.

MOOD

The mood of a room affects the way you feel in it. Although the architecture, proportions, and trim all contribute to the ambience, it is the details of the decor that really set the tone. The same Victorian home could look airy and light, intimate and cozy, or actually cluttered, depending upon the scale and colors of paper or fabric patterns chosen, whether the furnishings are pressed oak or massive upholstered pieces, whether the window treatments are velvet or lace, and the type and number of accessories—rugs, pictures, cushions, plants, and collectibles.

© Bradley Olman

What sort of mood do you wish to create in your bathroom? Ask yourself the following questions: Is it to be a space of relaxation and leisure, or one of clinical efficiency? Do you want it to feel like a conservatory, full of light and plants? Or would you prefer to be comfortably homey, with hearts, checks, and rustic country accessories? Will you give a nod to the Old World by choosing hand-painted tiles, wrought-iron fittings, and filet-crochet curtains? Is your taste eclectic, leading you toward stained glass and other artisan-made accoutrements? Have you always longed for a feminine boudoir, with lots of sheer draperies, pretty framed prints, silver toilet accessories, and an upholstered chair? Or do you prefer a more tailored environment?

TRADITIONAL OR CONTEMPORARY?

Chances are that the overall look of your bathroom will be either traditional, though not necessarily old, or contemporary. Traditional baths, such as the green-and-white room **at left**, tend to have freestanding fixtures. This is an older bathroom, with the original fixtures still in good condition and it is large enough to include a marble-topped bureau. The stenciling on the wood floor repeats the wallpaper pattern and masks the worn boards. Framed prints, flowers, white accessories, and the hand-painted posy on the tub combine to make the room look fresh and pretty.

In contrast, the fixtures in contemporary baths are built in. The quiet room **below** features a vanity set into a mirror-backed corner, a big stall shower, and a large tub dropped into a wide plat-

Courtesy of Kohler

© Jessie Walker Associates

form. The decor of this room is spare, with flat oak trim used to break up floor, door, and walls; note how the molding framing the mirror extends to finish the top of the shower stall yet still preserves the openness of the high ceiling.

Depending upon the choice of accoutrements, the mood of a traditional or contemporary bath can be elegant, formal, casual, country, austere, relaxing, or eclectic, but the contemporary bath is more likely to be clinical, high-tech, and dramatic, while the traditional lends itself more to the ornate, quaint, or intimate, like the pretty little bath **above**. Here a floral-patterned pedestal sink and

139

fully painted table, the tub, and the green potted plants stand out, evoking a mood of cool serenity.

The very contemporary bath **at right**, predominated by hard, shiny white surfaces, looks almost institutional. This room is typical of the spacious master baths being built today, with a whirlpool, a large separate shower, and a long two-basin vanity set into a mirrored alcove; the expanse of mirror makes the room seem lighter and wider than it really is. The shower stall is transparent, taking advantage of the light and the woodland view. With tile on the walls and floors, this room is fairly waterproof; the fan-light fixture near the shower helps to draw off steam. Interestingly, you might expect to find a more traditional bath in a home with divided-light windows, but the grid of the tile grout complements that of the window muntins, and the overall effect is not at all displeasing.

toilet are set against complementary tiles framed by generously proportioned white moldings; the solid walls offer some relief from the decorative patterning, and the soft drapery enhances the feminine mood. Architecturally, the room **above** is late-eighteenth-century English and could be original or reproduction; the fixtures are new, and the ornate pedestal sink lends an air of formality that is reiterated by the sconces, pendant light, draped valance and matching shower curtain, and, of course, the folding screen. Though the style of this room is rather grand for its size, the mood is mellow.

Of course, it is quite possible to give a traditional bath a clean, spare look, particularly if the room is large and left fairly unadorned. In the room **at right**, the footed tub is set against a bay of large windows; the sheer curtains, walls, hexagonal floor tiles, and rug are all pristine white, with the result that the fanci-

© William B. Seitz

have been broken in unexpected places, with the door and window extending above the top of the tile. The effect is quite striking, with the white molding that frames each element trimmed with simple squares that pick up the squareness of the white-grouted wall tiles. The mirrored wall above the vanity shares the same trim and reflects the tile. The paneled doors and coordinating vanity and tub surround continue the theme in a traditional cabinetry style. Note the choice of cream-colored paint for the upper walls and ceiling; it softens the overall effect.

Sometimes architectural style can really set a mood. The bathroom in the old stone house **at right** has a rustic ambience that is enhanced but not dependent upon the choice of fixtures; a new drop-in tub with a rough-sawn board surround would be as at home here as the old freestanding one. It is the naturally finished wood floor and ceiling and the stone and barn-board walls that set the tone. Most of the accessories are wood as well —the towel bars, mirror frame, and an eclectic assortment of small cabinets—and the braided rugs are right at home among them. If you love this look, think carefully before you choose it for your main bath; be sure that the room is well ventilated and con-

If the look of the previous bath is too clinical for you, perhaps you would prefer the mood of quiet elegance found in the room **above**. Here a mirror fills the wall above a gray-and-brown, marble-topped, raised-panel vanity. The under-mounted stainless steel sink is paired with chrome fittings and accessories, and the small geometric pattern chosen for the green wallpaper completes the tailored effect. While each of the elements chosen for this room has roots in previous periods of design, there is nothing old-fashioned about their disposition here.

At first glance, the green-tiled contemporary bathroom **at right** seems perfectly straightforward. It is indeed a very simple and rather austere room, but a closer look reveals that it was designed with careful attention to detail and proportion. Everything but the tub and the sink is rectilinear—including the glass shades in the Arts and Crafts–style sconces—but the angles

© image/dennis krukowski. Design:

sider sealing the wood if you live in a humid climate—this decor would not be easy to keep free of mildew.

Once you determine the mood and style that are appropriate for your lifestyle, you will be able to refine a floor plan and choose the specific fixtures and finishing touches that work in your space and budget. To help you pull your thoughts together, make a file of clippings from decorating magazines and bro-

chures from plumbing fixture manufacturers. Include anything that appeals to you; you may like a particular color combination, tile pattern, or window treatment, even if the room it is displayed in is too grand. Collect paint chips and fabric swatches, anything that suggests the look you think you want. When you are ready to refine your concept, you can edit the file until the look comes together.

143

FIXTURES AND FITTINGS

I t is quite possible that you have never really given much thought to plumbing fixtures and their fittings (controls), other than to appreciate the fact that they are there. Their existence, of course, is the reason that bathrooms are built. The mechanics of most plumbing fixtures are quite straightforward, so when you select them you will be more concerned with their size, style, and price than with the way they work, and you will find many options available. When you look for fixtures to complement the mood and style of your bath, be sure to consider the look of the fittings at the same time; the right fittings can imbue standard fixtures with special style, while the wrong ones can ruin an otherwise tasteful look.

PLUMBING FIXTURES

The first thing that may occur to you when you begin to choose the plumbing fixtures for your bathroom is that the array of models available is overwhelming, the specifications are confusing, and the prices are variable. Ideally, the fixtures you select will be with you for a long time, so let the choice be a thoughtful one. Before you can actually order fixtures, your floor plan must be complete (see chapter 7). However, having a good idea of the type of fixtures you want may help you to develop that plan, so it is not premature to check out the possibilities early in the design process. The type of bathroom you are designing also will influence the choice: master bath, full bath, or half bath or powder room.

If possible, visit dealers' showrooms to see what the fixtures really look like. Not only will this allow you to be sure you really like the styling, it is also a good way to pick up brochures with the size specifications and get an idea of price range. There is no rule that states that you must select all fixtures from the same manufacturer; this is only important if you are using a particular color or an ornamental or highly stylized line. In fact, you may find that the basin and tub sizes you need are available only from diverse sources; if this is the case, make sure the styling is compatible. If you do use fixtures from more than one manufacturer, check to be sure you will be able to use matching fittings with all of them, because not all fittings fit all fixtures.

Although the choices seem overwhelming at first, there are three criteria that will immediately limit them: style, price, and size.

Style

When you begin to look around, your understanding of the mood and style desired should be fairly clear. Are you interested in a traditional or contemporary bathroom? Do you want a wall-mounted, pedestal, or vanity sink? Do you prefer a tub/shower or separate tub and shower units? Are you looking for a standard toilet or a period one with a wall-mounted water tank and a pull chain? Does someone in your home use a wheelchair? Is it important in your community to use a water-saving model? How trendy is your taste? Bathroom fixtures tend to date, so be sure you really like what you are looking at, and consider whether the next owner of your home will be as fond of them as you are.

Price

When you consider the cost of plumbing fixtures, include the cost of installation—not because it will necessarily cost more to install one unit as opposed to another, but because the cost of repairing or replacing an existing one may be considerable, particularly for a tub or shower. Buy the best model that you can afford; a poorly made stall shower may leak so badly that not only will you have to replace it, you may have to repair structural or cosmetic damage caused by the errant water. Likewise, replacing a built-in tub almost always requires some tile work. Once you have an idea of the cost involved, consider only brands that fit within your budget; there is no point designing an entire room around something that you simply cannot afford. On the other hand, if you stick with a standard toilet and tub, you may be able to afford a beautifully detailed pedestal lavatory, or a floral-patterned basin.

Size

There is a bathroom fixture made to fit in nearly any imaginable space. If your room is large, you will have more models to choose from and may be able to include extras, such as a bidet, a larger vanity, or an exercise area. If your room is small or you are dealing with an oddly shaped space, however, the selection will be much smaller.

To avoid confusion while you are narrowing your fixture selection, make a file that includes only eligible models—those that meet your taste, budget, and space requirements. Unless your funds are unlimited, you will probably find that the contents of this file are manageable.

Material Matters

Whether you are planning a traditional or contemporary bathroom, you'll find that plumbing fixtures are made from a variety of materials. There are advantages to each, with differences in price and weight (be sure that the structure of the room is sufficient to support heavier fixtures) that may sway you one way or another.

Cast Iron or Steel

One of the most common materials for tubs and sinks is enameled (porcelain-surfaced) cast iron, which is durable, heavy, and available in many sizes, shapes, and colors, the last of which may vary from year to year. The surface is easy to keep clean, its only disadvantage being that it can chip if heavy metal objects are dropped in it. Enameled fixtures with damaged surfaces can be professionally resurfaced or you can do it yourself with a two-step epoxy kit available at most hardware stores. Refinished fixtures may not be as long-wearing as the original enamel, but they provide a durable and attractive solution that is cheaper than replacement. Fixtures made of enameled steel are also available; they are less expensive than those of cast iron, but tend to be less insulating and noisier.

Vitreous China and Pottery

Vitreous china is the standard material for toilets, bidets, and pedestal and wall-mounted sinks; it is very often used for vanity sinks as well.

The fixtures are cast in molds and can have virtually any shape. The china is heavy and durable, although it can chip if dropped or otherwise abused.

Vitreous china comes in many colors, which may vary from one year to the next. Some of the more expensive lines feature decorative surface patterns. These can provide a key or theme to the room's decor, permitting an ambience in which the fixtures are neither stark nor clinical. The charming room **below** is a wonderful blend of Old World sensibilities. The toilet, lavatory,

Courtesy of Kohler

Courtesy of Kohler

and water reservoir have a floral pattern reminiscent of fine faience; the complementary wall painting and stenciled border edging the floor complete the mood of contemplative elegance. The blue-and-white pedestal sink **above**, with its fluted profile, controlled patterning, and elegant fittings, has a modern and formal demeanor; the slick (and protective) tiled alcove in which it sits is softened by the trellis-patterned wallpaper. In addition to these attractive stock models, there are also limited-edition and one-of-a-kind ceramic sinks available through decorators and individual potters.

Fiberglass, Acrylic, and Solid Synthetic Materials

Molded fiberglass and acrylic are other common materials for built-in tubs and showers. In addition to basic tubs, these materials are available as one-piece tub/showers or stall showers,which being seamless, do not leak. Molded tubs and showers come in a variety of shapes and sizes; some tubs and shower bases are available with variously styled doors and molded surrounds (wall panels). The panels are made from solid synthetic materials with surfaces that match the base or simulate tile or stone. In addition, some solid synthetics are available as sheet goods for custom shower-wall installations. The wall-panel kits are easy to install and can usually go directly over existing tile.

Molded fiberglass and acrylic tubs and showers often include handy shelves, soap dishes, and safety handholds; some models even have seats. The all-white model **at right** is a straightforward example that is easy to picture in a new or remodeled bath. Fiberglass, cast acrylic, and solid synthetics are durable and easy to care for.

Molded solid synthetic materials are also used to make vanity basins. These materials are more familiar when identified by their brand names, for example, Corian and Nevamar. Solid synthetics are available in a wide range of colors and patterns, many of which simulate marble and other stones that are popular today. Unlike marble, they are very easy to care for and repair, should the surfaces be damaged.

Courtesy of Kohler

Tile and Marble

While tile and marble come to mind as the classic wallcoverings for built-in tub/shower units, it is quite possible to have both tubs and showers completely lined with either material. This requires careful planning, as the understructure must be correctly prepared, but depending upon the specific material and size, it does not have to be costly; your builder or tile vendor can explain the process to you. **On the left of page 149** is a marvelous large shower lined with a simple but striking geometric mosaic. Some tile manufacturers will lay out your mosaic pattern of one- or two-inch (2.5 or 5cm) tiles on mesh sheets that are about one foot (0.3m) square so that it is no more complicated to install than any other tile. Remarkably, this attractive pattern uses only three colors. Note the built-in tiled shelves.

The advantages of a tile- or marble-lined tub or shower are various: they can be built to almost any shape, they can include simple or complex mosaic patterns, and they can appear extremely luxurious. The disadvantages are that they are very heavy, the slightest error in framing can throw off a mosaic pattern, and the surfaces are somewhat more difficult to maintain

© image/dennis krukowski, Design:

trouble locating a metal countertop lavatory that is to your liking, you can consider a kitchen or bar sink, or ask to see the institutional section of a manufacturer's catalog.

While neither commonplace nor inexpensive, lavatories and tubs (including whirlpools) are available in wood. Be sure you understand their maintenance before you purchase one.

Tubs and Showers

The relative grandeur of the bathroom you are creating will influence your selection of tub and shower. If you are planning a child's or guest's bath, or if the room is on the small side, you will most likely want a combined tub/shower unit. If, however, you are planning a master bath, you may follow the fashion of the moment with a luxuriously large tub and separate stall shower like those in the cathedral-ceilinged room **on page 150**, which is designed to provide privacy while maximizing the daylight.

Courtesy of Kallista Inc.

than porcelain or fiberglass, particularly if your water is hard. If you are trying to fit a shower into a small bathroom, you might consider treating the room like one big tiled shower stall—with a drain in the floor and a curtain available to keep the water off the toilet and sink.

Polished Metal and Wood Admittedly, the era when the big tin washtub was a regular Saturday feature is gone from most parts of the world, and you are more likely to find stainless steel lining the kitchen sink than the bathtub. But if you have a yearning for bygone style with present-day plumbing, it can be satisfied. Take, for example, the very elegant copper tub **at right**, which comes complete with hand-held shower.

Countertop lavatories can be made of polished metal, with stainless steel being the most commonly available. If you have

© Melabee Miller/Envision

can be any distance from the walls. There is a lip at the perimeter of the tub that sits over the platform, preventing seepage. None of the exterior sides of this type of tub is finished, although a separate side piece, or apron, is available with some models; the top and freestanding sides of the platform can be finished in a variety of ways. If the platform around a drop-in tub is more than a few inches wide, there is usually a step or two built along one side so that it will be easy and safe to climb in and out of the tub. Built-in tubs can also be sunk below the floor if there is space underneath the bathroom, and this is a good option for a tub going under the eaves. Some built-in tubs come with holes for the faucet and controls; some offer placement options for these to accommodate different installations. Other tubs are designed to be used with wall-mounted fittings.

A whirlpool is a tub with an electric pump that circulates the water through multiple jets in the sidewalls. Many whirlpools are large enough to accommodate several people at once, but they come in standard tub sizes as well. Whirlpools are available in either of the built-in styles, and some manufacturers make molded tub/shower whirlpools.

Both tubs and whirlpools come in a variety of shapes—oblong, oval, round, and hourglass—and there are even models designed to fit into corners. If you like to read in the tub or take long relaxing baths, you should try to select your tub from a showroom where you can climb in and test the models for comfort. While some of the styles are quite ornate, a simple one can be just as impressive if it is integrated thoughtfully into the rest of the decor, as is the whirlpool **at right**. Here, the clean lines of the fixture are strikingly framed by handsome glazed tiles set in white grout, which ties the tub to the rest of the room. The wide-mouthed faucet is dramatic without being fussy.

Tub Styles Bathtubs come in many sizes; in North America the preference is for those that are long enough to recline in, while in other parts of the world they are frequently shorter and deeper—called hip baths—sometimes with a seat molded in. Bathtubs are available as freestanding and as built-in units. Freestanding tubs often sit on feet, and their exterior is finished on all sides; the old-fashioned claw-footed variety is often deeper than the new built-in models. Extra-long and extra-deep tubs are sometimes available from the major manufacturers but are not displayed or promoted by local dealers. Be sure to ask about other sizes that can be specially ordered from the factory.

There are two types of built-in tubs. One type can be installed in an alcove or corner fitted with a shower head; these usually have one or two (adjacent) finished exterior sides. The other type, called self-rimming, can be dropped into a platform, which

Shower Styles While any watertight area with a drain can be made into a shower, showers fall into two basic categories: tub and stall. Built-in alcove or corner tubs almost always have a

Courtesy of Kallista Inc.

shower fixture installed on one wall. These usually have a curtain to keep the water out of the rest of the room, but doors are also an option. Freestanding tubs can have shower fixtures above as well, and there are a variety of ring-shaped rods that can be hung from the ceiling so that they can be curtained. However, because there is usually a point of conflict between the shower controls and the overlap of the curtain, these tend to be less than ideally waterproof.

Stall showers have a shallow watertight base, called a dish, but they are not usually intended to hold still water the way a tub is. They can accommodate one or more people at a time, depending upon their size. Stall showers are commonly built into either a corner or an alcove and are usually entered by a door rather than through a curtain. The door and any freestanding walls of contemporary stall showers are often transparent; there are many styles and sizes available, either paired with a molded dish or meant to be installed on a custom tiled base. The one shown **below** is clean and sophisticated; the clear glass in the brass-finished frame shows off the marble-lined corner and complementary shower fittings and adds no weight to the room. One other option is an inexpensive all-in-one enameled metal shower stall (the kind that has a curtained doorway); these are easy to install but tend to leak and rust.

Lavatories

Bathroom sinks and basins, properly and more elegantly referred to as lavatories, also come in a variety of styles and sizes. There are lavatories that will fit into corners, tiny ones that help to squeeze a powder room into a closet, models big enough to bathe an infant in, and everything in between. Bathroom lavatories are usually oblong, round, or oval, but they are occasionally triangular or hexagonal. Lavatories fall into three basic styles: wall-mounted, pedestal, or countertop.

Wall-Mounted Lavatories

Before vanity cabinets became common in the middle of this century, wall-mounted lavatories were the standard in all but the most elegant bathrooms. Their styling ranges from nostalgic to sleekly contemporary, their size from petite to generous. Some are no more than a simple basin with a ledge or backsplash to accommodate the controls, while others are substantial enough to hold soaps and other toilet accessories. The chief disadvantages to a wall-mounted lavatory are that the water- and drainpipes are exposed, the space below is useless, and the surrounding walls and floor are easily splashed. Though not usually the fixture of choice in a contemporary bath, a small wall-mounted lavatory requires a minimum of space and may be the only alternative in a very small room.

Pedestal Lavatories

Pedestal lavatories almost always convey an aura of elegance or formality. Because the water- and drainpipes are concealed by the base, they impart a finished look to a traditional bathroom. Some new models have elaborate decorative moldings; some, like the handsome one **at upper right**, are reminiscent of nineteenth- and early-twentieth-century styles; and some are sleekly contemporary. Although they are larger than the smallest wall-mounted lavatories, they are available in many sizes. Because the various styles feature differing backsplash and edge configurations, shop carefully to allows. Countertop lavatories can be mounted under the countertop, dropped into it, or if the counter is composed of solid synthetic material, molded in one with it. For the convenience of people in wheelchairs, there are specially designed sinks that extend beyond the front of the cabinet.

For aesthetic reasons, the material you choose for a countertop lavatory will depend upon the style of cabinetry you are using and the mood that you wish to establish. A simple white basin is never out of place; if this idea appeals to you, you should have no difficulty finding one that meets your style and budgetary criteria. If, however, you yearn for something special, you might consider something like the fluted and brilliantly enameled blue basin **below**. It is not necessary to have grand cabinetry when you select a basin of such importance—this one is mounted under a simple white counter—but you probably want to pair it with equally stylish fittings. Some of the decoratively patterned china

Courtesy of Kohler

Courtesy of Kohler

be sure that the model you select will accommodate adequate toilet accessories and that the proportions of the pedestal are pleasing to your eye. Some models are actually composed of a wall-mounted basin with a separate pedestal; others are freestanding. The chief drawbacks to pedestal sinks are that the space under the basin is useless and the surrounding walls and floor are easily splashed.

Countertop Lavatories

Vanity cabinets first came into use for functional reasons: they provide under-sink storage and minimize errant water damage. Today, they tend to be as large as space permits and as elaborate as taste decrees and budget

Courtesy of Antique Faucets

lavatories, like the blue-and-white one **above**, are available with coordinating fittings. Note how thoughtfully this charming basin, with its pattern of fanciful bunnies and foliage, is set into a white-tiled countertop and paired with a backsplash of coordinating tiles balanced by a dark blue bead.

Toilets

Standard model, high tank, low tank, concealed tank, water-saving, and silent flush are all options that you can consider when shopping for a toilet. Water-saving models, like the one **at upper right**, are soon to be mandatory in many areas. There are even models whose flush is activated when the lid is closed, intended to cure chronic offenders in seat-up battles. Although you may never have thought about it, toilets also come in various sizes and pedestal shapes; this feature can be crucial if your bathroom is small.

Bidets

Bidets are far less common in North America than in Europe. Many manufacturers feature bidets that coordinate with the toilets in their higher-priced fixture lines, and as they should be installed side by side, a matched set will look best. Bidets are connected with both hot and cold water supply lines, a pop-up drain so the bowl can be filled with water, and in some models, a sprayer in the base of the bowl for personal hygiene.

FIXTURE FITTINGS

Bathroom fittings are refinements, giving focus to the room design and revealing or establishing its true character. Even a classic, inherently plain all-white tub/shower like the one **at right** can assume an aura of sophisticated grace if it is finished

with elegant fittings. Those used here have classic lines and a brilliant gold finish, which carry over to the utility basket and the curtain rod. The choice of a white curtain helps to focus the eye and reinforces the successfully understated but tasteful treatment.

Fittings are available in a myriad of styles, which in turn come in a wide array of finishes. You can choose among nostalgic antique styles or voluptuous or streamlined modern ones; pick something understated or something dramatic; add polish with a bright gold, brass, or chrome finish or patina with a soft one; make a romantic statement with floral-patterned, china-trimmed knobs; or strike an up-beat note with brightly hued plastic. There are controls that push, turn, or lift. Shower fittings can be hand-held or fixed to the wall; some even massage or have adjustable sprays. There are classic faucets, and widespread faucets, spouts, and sprays. If you are in doubt, pick something

with classic lines, like the timeless shower heads and mixer **below**, for a traditional bath, or choose something industrial and clean-lined, like the widespread bath faucet and sophisticated shower system **at right**, for a contemporary one.

Bathroom fittings are functional as well as decorative. The knobs, faucets, and drains that you see are only part of what you shop for; they are sold as sets with the couplings and castings necessary to connect them to the water supply and drainpipes, which account for some of their often substantial cost. Toilets are sold with the trip lever (flush handle) in place, but without the seat. All the fittings for all other fixtures must be purchased separately. The more elaborate your bathroom— whirlpool, multiple shower heads, two-basin vanity—the more fittings you will require. And though many styles are available, all fittings are not the same size and they are not necessarily interchangeable. The specifications for each fixture indicate which

Courtesy of Kallista

COLD   HOT

KALLISTA

OFF

Courtesy of Kallista

Courtesy of Kallista

Courtesy of Kohler

fittings can be used with it; be sure you understand them before purchasing either fixtures or fittings. The fittings can easily be as expensive as the fixtures they adorn, so include them in your budget.

The style of the fittings should be compatible with that of the fixtures you use, so at least begin to shop for them at the same time. Many fixture manufacturers offer appropriate fittings, which can simplify the process, and there are independent brands of fittings as well. Price and quality are not necessarily linked, so check with your plumbing contractor to be sure the brand you are considering wears well.

CABINETRY AND COUNTERTOPS

The amount of cabinetry in a bathroom will depend upon the size of the room and whether built-in or freestanding fixtures are used. A traditional bath may have nothing more than a medicine cabinet; a powder room with a mirror over the sink may have none at all. But a new and very contemporary master bath is likely to have a two-basin vanity and perhaps even linen storage and a concealed washer and dryer as well.

The first function of cabinetry is storage. Because bathrooms are self-contained and space is often of a premium, it is a good idea to approach all your storage spaces with the same aesthetic eye, planning cabinets, closet doors, and any other items, such as bookcases, in the same or complementary designs. When initially determining the style of cabinetry to use, refer to the architecture of the room. Is there decorative wood molding or wainscoting? You may wish to use wood cabinets, and paint or finish them to match. Is the door to the room of raised-panel construction? Perhaps the cabinet doors should be also. Are the lines of the room angular and sleek? If so, consider European-style cabinets (with the doors flush, the case concealed), finished with a laminate or perhaps lacquered. Is the space dramatic? Perhaps cabinetry with a sweeping curve is in order. If so, it could be topped with marble or one of the solid synthetic materials—these are ideal for curved areas because their edges need no applied facing. Are you a flea-market junkie with a collection of old marble sinks and counters just waiting for bases? Is built-in cabinetry really the answer? A traditional bath in a turn-of-the-century summer home might feel lighter and airier with a wicker cupboard. Consider what the overall effect is likely to be, as well as your budget: will you be having fine custom cabinets built or are you relying on stock units from a lumberyard or home center? If you are redoing an existing bath, do you need to replace the cabinets, or can you refinish—or faux-finish—them and replace just the countertop?

As your cabinets begin to take shape in your imagination, the materials from which they will be made come immediately to mind. In all likelihood, the cabinets will be wood with a clear or painted finish, or laminate-surfaced; they might also be built of one of the solid synthetic materials. The countertops may be one of these materials, or they can be composed of tile or a slab of marble or other stone. Think of the mood and style you wish to create: the cabinetry will play a major role in establishing them, and it in turn will dictate which materials to select.

Traditional raised-panel cabinetry provides ample storage in the all-white room **on page 158**. The mood here is very different from that of the slick all-white bath on page 141. This bathroom, while unpretentious, is quietly elegant and has many thoughtful details. The closet doors repeat the styling of the vanity, which has two self-rimming lavatories dropped into a plastic laminate–surfaced counter. With the frameless mirrors reflecting the unbroken white surfaces, the room appears bigger than it is. The pretty wall sconces and small white knobs are decorative without being heavy, and the black accents (note the wrought-iron towel bar) are striking but not overwhelming.

Cabinets such as the ones in this bathroom are often available as stock units, with different components that can be configured to meet many needs and fit many spaces. Plastic laminate surfaces are available in a multitude of colors and patterns and can be easily glued to a substrate structural material. They are flexible and can be wrapped over curved surfaces, such as at the front edge of this counter. Early laminates were composed of a brown or black core with a very thin layer of the color or pattern topping one side, resulting in a dark line marking any exposed edges (such as the end of a countertop), but because they are now available with the color penetrating the entire thickness, this is no longer a problem. Laminates can be applied to cabinet cases and doors—or other upright surfaces—as well as to countertops. They are durable, relatively inexpensive, and easy to care for. They can, however, be permanently marred with nicks or burns.

The beautiful custom-built cabinet at the end of the oddly shaped room **at upper right** is impressive; its design both acknowledges and relieves the long, narrow proportions of the space. There are a number of good ideas at work here. Only the left-hand section is functional, while the panels on the right are simply decorative. The curved niche provides a handsome setting for a favorite treasure and is thoughtfully echoed by the fixed panel to its right; although these lead your eye upward, they minimize the loftiness of the ceiling. Note the use of center-

© image/dennis krukowski, Design:

opening doors on the cupboard; a single panel would not be able to clear the fixture in front of it. The wood-grain pattern on the wallpaper and the stained wood floor continue the motif of the curly maple woodwork, and the wide white baseboard complements the pristine fixtures.

The unusual wall-mounted vanity in the duplex bathroom **at right** is made of a white solid synthetic material; the basin is integral with the top, and there is a deep drawer cut into the apron. This unusual room is tucked dramatically under the eaves. The embellishments are very uncomplicated, the mood rather Oriental. The skylit tub, plain gray carpeting, clean-lined vanity, and simply framed mirror let the space speak for itself.

Solid synthetics are composed of the same material all the way through and can be cut, glued, sanded and polished, and repaired or repolished in the same way that a natural material like wood or marble can be. Solid synthetics are sturdy enough

160

to be worked alone and do not need to be glued to a substrate. They come in many patterns and colors and are available in sheets of several thicknesses and in a variety of shapes; some custom fabrications can be arranged with the manufacturer. Solid synthetics are not inexpensive, but they are extremely durable, stain-resistant, and easy to care for.

It may be that you are already working with a number of materials in one bath, and when you get to the cabinetry, are looking for a way to tie them together. The multilevel bathroom **at right** is paved with marble and lined with ceramic tile. Space is fairly tight in this room, there is not much daylight, and with all the different levels—the window in the shower, the jutting vanity, the tall mirror, and the high ceilings—there is a lot going on. With the same tile and marble used to face the vanity, which might have seemed blocky in another material, the room maintains its integ-

© Daniel Eifert, Design: Bogdanow & Associates, Architects

© William B. Seitz

rity. The richly grained doors provide a subtle contrast, and the white knobs echo the controls on the fixtures. Note the use of the aqua tile bead, which complements the green-and-white color scheme, provides a decorative accent, and frames the mirror. Note also the wise use of mable on the windowsill. Windows in showers are always problematic, but this one is well curtained and the marble slab, having no grout lines, is less prone to damage from standing water than tile would be.

Bathroom cabinetry can also be topped with ceramic tile, which offers many design possibilities. You could pick solid colors and arrange them in a checkerboard or other mosaic pattern, or select one or more of the many charming hand-painted patterns. If you are using tile for a tub surround or the floors and

under-mounted basin tops a sleek white vanity. The brass fittings complement the warm tone of the stone. The mirrored wall above the vanity makes the room seem larger, and because the expanse is unbroken, the effect is particularly uncluttered. Painting the louvered closet doors to match the vanity helps to tie them together; pinstripe wallpaper completes the tailored look and unifies the whole room. The treatment of this room is really very simple, and it is not difficult to imagine adapting it to update a bathroom that is tired but not in need of total renovation.

walls, you may wish to repeat or complement it on the countertops. Tiles come in a variety of sizes and profiles; most lines include beads, bull noses, and corner pieces so that backsplashes and edges can be covered if desired. Pick the tile and plan the arrangement before finalizing your cabinetry so that you can be sure that it will fit as desired. If you are planning to tile a vanity top, you should use a self-rimming lavatory.

If you are planning a tailored bathroom, consider keeping the cabinetry very simple, and dressing it up with a sophisticated countertop. In the room **above**, a rich granite slab with an

© image/dennis krukowski. Design:

Courtesy of Kohler

Natural stone slabs—whether marble, travertine, limestone, granite, or slate—make great countertops. They come in many colors, are often beautifully grained, can be cut to shape, and can be polished or not as you wish. Granite is fairly impervious to stains, while marble and slate can be sealed for protection. Each stone has its own care requirements, so check with your vendor to be sure you understand them; if the maintenance sounds like too much trouble, you can decide to go for the well-loved and worn look, but be aware that this is not easy to remove. The different stones carry very different price tags. They are priced by the square foot (or square meter), and the price usually includes cutting and polishing, with an extra charge for a bull nose or other profile on the edge, but be sure to verify that. Stone slabs are heavy, so the cabinetry and floor must be sturdy enough to support them. If you are building your own cabinets, it is a wise idea to have the stone vendor come to measure for the countertop; that way, you will not be responsible for any error, should one occur.

If you have a passion for beautiful wood, you might consider using it for the countertop as well as the cabinet base. Because all bathroom surfaces are likely to get wet and water is an enemy of wood, you should be sure to seal and finish such a counter-top properly, paying particular attention to the cutout edge. The fanciful lavatory in the little powder room **at left** is dropped into a beautiful rosewood countertop. Coordinating ceramic tiles front the apron and trim the backsplash. Perhaps you yearn for even more formality? Consider a freestanding vanity cabinet such as the one **at right**, which looks very elegant paired with the classi-cal mirror and striped paper with garland borders. Cabinets such as this are perhaps not suited to the everyday bath, but they are available from better furniture makers. Some of the fix-ture manufacturers also offer console vanities, which feature a lavatory set into a small countertop with legs at the front corners. Or if you have a bureau or dressing table that conveys exactly the right mood, you can have a good carpenter convert it to accommodate a lavatory and plumbing.

Courtesy of Kohler

163

WALLCOVERINGS AND FLOORING

Choosing wall and floor coverings for a bathroom is a more complicated process than just deciding upon a color scheme and determining whether or not wallpaper and carpeting will suit, as you might for a living room, dining room, or bedroom. Bathrooms get wet and steamy, and water, while kind to the body, can wreak havoc on paint, paper, and wood. Add humidity to the environment, and creeping black mildew may spread its sometimes irradicable shadow over walls, ceilings, and floors. Ceramic or stone tiles look fabulous and are long-wearing, but they are also cold underfoot and can be slippery when wet. Fortunately, there are good-looking, decorative, and water-resistant options for durable wall and floor finishes. In fact, almost any aesthetic whim, from the classic and straightforward to the witty or eclectic, can be satisfied.

While the desired mood and style of your room will influence your choice of wall and floor coverings, there are so many pattern and color options available in most materials that you can be guided by budgetary, installation, and maintenance requirements as much as by decorative criteria. If you want solid color, you can choose paint or tile; if you prefer pattern, you can select paper, tile, or stone, or create your own decorative surface with paint.

If humidity is not a threat, fabric can adorn walls and windows. Unless splashing children are likely to leave large puddles, water-tolerant carpeting can cover the floor. If you wish to make the room seem larger, be lavish with mirrors (but don't be surprised by your own reflection). The important thing is to understand the options so that you can put them to use effectively.

Color value can affect the perceived size of a room; light or pale colors will make a space seem larger, while dark or deep colors will make it seem smaller. Colors can look very different in different lighting situations or in combination with one another, so test samples of paint, wallpaper, or tile in your room by daylight and by artificial light to be sure that the effect is what you have in mind.

Fortunately, most wall and floor treatments can be easily installed and replaced. This is not to imply that you should select them casually knowing that mistakes can be corrected, but that when it is time for a fresh look, you may need to do no more than retile or change the wallpaper. While it is never convenient to take a bathroom out of service, it is far less disruptive to make these essentially cosmetic changes than to rip out all fixtures and start completely fresh.

However, if you are building anew, consider the longevity of the treatments you are leaning toward. Tile—whether vinyl, rubber, or ceramic—is usually long-wearing, so you would be wise to spend the extra money for the kind you really like. If you can't afford a whole room of hand-painted ceramic tiles, consider just a border of them. On the other hand, if the treatment you yearn for is really beyond your reach at the present, try to come up with an alternative that can be easily added to or replaced. For instance, you could tile only the tub alcove at first and paint the remaining walls; then when money permits, you could tile the painted walls.

PAINT AND VARNISH

There is a good chance that all but the fanciest marble-covered bathrooms will include some painted surfaces. Walls, wood floors, and trim can all be painted easily and beautifully, though the surfaces will not be as long-wearing as those that are tiled; there is no reason to reject paint just because it is an inexpensive and obvious idea. In fact, if you want to create a mood that is clean and simple, for instance in a Shaker-style home, paint may be ideal for everything but the shower surround. Avoid using matte-finish paints in the bathroom, as they are difficult to clean. High-gloss paints attract condensation, so limit them to trim and cabinetry; semi-gloss, eggshell, or satin-finish paints are most suitable for walls. If you wish to paint a wood floor, use porch or deck paints, which are formulated to withstand lots of moisture and traffic. Oil paints dry with a harder surface than latex or acrylic epoxy ones, but the latter expand and contract more easily with changes in heat and humidity; ask your vendor or a professional for advice on what type would be most suitable for your situation.

If you prefer a clear finish for wood surfaces, there are a variety of varnishes available for trim, cabinetry, or floors, many of which are plastic-based. If you want to change the color of the wood with stain, do so before applying a clear finish.

VINYL, CERAMIC, AND STONE

The least expensive and easiest-care bathroom floor covering is probably vinyl or rubber tiles or sheet goods. Both come in a great variety of colors and patterns, some of which simulate more expensive painted ceramic or veined stone surfaces. Different tiles can be combined to create checkerboards or other geometric designs. Sheet goods are manufactured in widths of 6 and 12 feet (2 and 4m), so it is often possible to install them without any seams, a boon in wet bathrooms. Vinyl and rubber flooring can both be installed by novice but handy homeowners.

© Bradley Olman

dow fill the white room with sunlight; this is a simply decorated but refreshing space.

It is very easy to develop an interesting geometric border when you work with solid-color tiles. The ubiquitous checkerboard springs immediately to mind, but the variations are really endless, particularly if you work with units of different shapes as well as different colors. In the room **at left**, small black tiles set in black grout form a grid on a ground of white octagonal tiles. There is a stylized black-and-white checkerboard border strikingly delineated by a bright red band. Ceramic tiles can be cut to follow almost any outline, and effects like this are not difficult to achieve. If you plan to install your own tile, just give yourself plenty of time and extra pieces for practice.

Ceramic tile is available in a variety of molding profiles as well as differently shaped flat pieces, so it is an excellent choice for finishing an irregularly shaped area. In the upstairs bath **below**, a tub has been set into a dormer with a window. The problem of

Because of its obvious water-shedding qualities, ceramic tile has for centuries been the covering of choice for bathroom walls and floors. The early civilizations in the Mediterranean basin excelled in decorative tile work, and if you think of the ancient Greeks and Romans in their baths, elegant rooms come to mind. In the Middle East, tile patterns followed a geometric inventiveness that has remained magical and inspiring to this day.

While conventional residential baths are rarely so exotic, thoughts of classic bathrooms almost always call forth images of white fixtures and cleanly tiled surfaces, like those of the lovely Old World bath on page 136, which has a high tiled dado—a traditional wall finish in rooms with showerless tubs—below the mural and a gracefully patterned tile floor. The airy old-fashioned bathroom **at left** features a combination of white wood and tile surfaces; here the dado is painted wainscoting topped with a molded rail, and the hexagonal floor tiles are accented by dark grout. The skylight above the tub and the prettily curtained win-

fit has been solved with a platform step and an array of handy ledges. The tidiness of the arrangement is emphasized by the black tiles outlining each dimension and the witty mosaic bath mat, which catches any water that strays from the curtainless shower. Handsome black towel bars complement the effect. The window curtain provides privacy from neighbors and also protects the wooden window trim from water damage—always an issue with shower windows. The top of this window is removed from the path of the spray, but should you have to deal with one that is not, try to use a rustproof curtain rod. These are not easy to find; a wooden dowel will also work—either on its own or slid into a length of flexible chrome supply piping (available at a plumbing supply or hardware store).

If you wish to create a sophisticated atmosphere that is smooth and clean without being sterile, you might consider lining an entire bathroom with stone pavers (tiles), and accenting it with the color found in the veining. The very contemporary black-and-white room **at left** has a custom-built tub lined inside and out with marble, which covers the floor and walls as well. The lacquered black vanity and generous mirror continue the sleek, formal mood. The carpet is a relief from all the hard surfaces—it also absorbs water and sound—but maintains the mood with its generous black border. Note the interesting use of the interior window framed in the mirror: the shirred curtains maintain privacy while still permitting conversation with someone in the dressing room beyond.

Marble or other stone pavers can be combined very effectively with other materials. Not only is this less expensive than lining an entire room with them, it also allows you to develop a mood that is not quite so slick. The small bath in the apartment **at upper right** has a high dado of the same green-veined marble that covers the floor. The paneled apron fronting the tub picks up the same cool sea-foam tints, which are repeated on the window and inset shelf trim. The window has an unobstructed view of a distant city skyline; because there is no chance of neighbors peeping, it can remain uncurtained.

© image/dennis krukowski, Design:

This room very successfully combines the contemporary and traditional: new fixtures, classic cabinetry, and timeless marble work together to achieve an unpretentious elegance.

Deciding to use marble or one of the other stones as a floor or wallcovering opens up a world of choices; you have to pick not only the color, but also the density of the veining, which can have an equal effect on the final mood. When viewed at any distance, the color contrast derived from fine and even veining will mute and blend in a quiet demeanor, while a bold pattern will hold its own and dominate all but the most palatial spaces. If your room is very small, think carefully about how you will feel confronting spectacularly swirled walls while making your early

Courtesy of Kohler

Although the previous room is truly grand, the inset shower is something to consider in any home that has the space to accommodate it. Inset showers keep water and steam well contained, and the minimal framing of the glass doors keeps most models from being obtrusive, making them compatible with various styles of architecture. The one in the Southwestern-style house at **lower right** is nearly identical to the marble-trimmed one mentioned above, but the setting and mood couldn't be more different. While the shower itself is lined with tile, the rest of the room has the textured plaster walls typical of adobe or Mediterranean-style homes. The monochrome ocher walls are quiet and restful, an inexpensive, simple, and very appropriate choice in any dry, sun-beaten climate.

WALLPAPER AND FABRIC

Ceramic tile and marble, no matter how beautiful, inevitably have a certain coldness as wallcoverings; paint, in addition to not always being practical, is sometimes just too plain to impart a particular spirit or mood. For these reasons, you may want to consider covering some or all of your bathroom walls with wallpaper or fabric, which are available in a nearly infinite variety of patterns and colors. Scrubbable vinyl "papers" are ideal for use in particularly steamy bathrooms or in those where little folk may leave handprints on their way to the tub. In well-ventilated baths, and certainly in half-baths or powder rooms, conventional wallpaper can be used without problems. Fabric can be applied taut like wallpaper or allowed to hang freely from the top of the wall. Both wallpaper and fabric can be easily installed by the homeowner, and there are many books and videos available that explain the various techniques; check your local library and video rental stores.

As you consider wallpaper or fabric patterns, keep in mind the mood and style of your room. There are reproduction patterns appropriate for older homes, classic patterns that work in many environments, and all sorts of contemporary prints that range

morning toilet. If your room is larger, that may be just what you are looking for to imbue it with drama. The contemporary bath **above** makes good use of boldly figured marble by combining it with an equally grand checkerboard floor and then breaking it up with smaller checkered bands. The very contemporary inset shower continues the theme. It is not hard to imagine yourself in an ancient elegant palazzo on some exotic coast.

from the sophisticated to the downright funky. Additionally, there are many charming juvenile prints, should you be doing an exclusively children's bath. There are florals and figuratives, stripes, checks and other geometrics, trompe l'oeil patterns, and more. Among all of these are new and traditional colorations and a range of proportions. Many manufacturers produce coordinated lines, with prints and geometrics in a variety of scales designed to work together; these sometimes include narrow borders that can add interest to walls or coordinating fabrics that can be used for draperies or shower curtains.

The print you choose for a wallcovering can do more than create an attractive background. Depending upon its color and scale, it can make the walls advance or recede, add or subtract light, or convey peace or energy. And the particular print will do much to establish a mood, be it romantic, feminine, tailored, or exotic. A printed wallcovering can also pick up a theme or leitmotif that is appropriate to the use, location, or owner of the room;

© image/dennis krukowski. Design:

Courtesy of Kohler

shells and other seaside images are common bathroom motifs. The room **above** above takes this idea a step further. The owner's love of sailing is reflected in the nautical charts that line the walls and the backsplash of delft tiles painted with ships under full sail. The curtain draped at the window sports a pattern of twisted ropes. There is nothing campy about this room. It is understated and serene; the cabinetry, sconces, and mirror are rather formal, and the mood is relaxing—and intriguing. It is not difficult to imagine achieving a similar look with road maps for a great traveler, theater programs, or even magazine covers. Any of these nontraditional wallpapers should be sealed with a coat of non-yellowing varnish, such as an interpenetrating polymer, to increase their longevity. One word of caution: paper glued to the wall cannot be removed without damage, so don't be tempted to paste up valuable old maps or prints.

Choosing one print and using a lot of it can make a room look cozy and intimate, particularly if the room has odd angles that might be disruptive if called to attention. The bath **above** doubles as a dressing room and wears an air of exotic mystery; this could be the garret so important to struggling writers of a bygone era. Everything but the floor and window has been covered in a rosy allover print fabric. The generously ruched skirts around the tub and sink subdue the glare of white fixtures (this is also a good way to hide worn fixtures or unsightly pipes). A tweed carpet covers the floor and is topped with a Chinese area rug. No attempt has been made to pretend that this is a sunny space; only a bit of light struggles through the window, but small shaded lamps shed an intimate glow where needed. The dark wood, ornate eclectic furnishings, and framed artwork live comfortably against the busily patterned walls. The owner of this room no doubt has a witty, self-assured sense of style.

Although the blue-and-white paper chosen for the Victorian-era bath **at upper right** is no less busy, the room is of such lofty proportions, and is so uncluttered and airy, that there is no hint of the close mystery of the garret above. This floral is of large enough scale to hold its own in the room but is not big enough to dominate or overwhelm. It has been edged with a lacelike

border (note the careful mitering at corners), and the effect is rather as though the room were papered with a large and lovely bandanna. The sheer curtains hanging in the leaded windows, the sparkling white trim, the wonderful vintage tub, and the braided rug laid over the soft white carpet all work to make this a most refreshing place. The soft patina of the mirror frame, pipes, and fittings adds sophistication and keeps the room from being too girlish. The nineteenth-century fashion plates, the comfortable wicker chair, and the waiting linens lend a femininity to the mood—it is pleasant to picture this as a home in a prosperous town somewhere in turn-of-the-century America.

MIRROR AND STAINED GLASS

Not all homes are blessed with such spacious proportions that we can stand a tub in isolation in the middle of a room. One very effective way to seemingly expand a small room is to line one or more walls with mirrors, extending real space through illusion. Glass mirror gives the truest reflection and is the easiest to maintain, but it fogs easily in steamy conditions. There are various

plastic mirrors that do not attract condensation, but they scratch easily and must be cleaned carefully. Be aware that any mirror that is installed within a shower area will become clouded with soap residue, which is very difficult to remove.

Using stained glass at the bathroom window is a wonderful way to ensure privacy; in the pretty cream room **below**, it assures that neighbors will have something lovely to look at but eliminates chance prying. Stained glass is elegant and, if colorful, can lend a wash of jewel tones when the sunlight filters through it; if placed opposite a large mirror, its beauty will be magnified—and it will frame whomever stands at the looking glass. Stained glass not only prevents others from seeing in, it also blocks your view and is a good solution to an unsightly or too-close prospect. Stained glass most often has to be custom made, but careful shopping at an architectural salvage or antique shop will sometimes yield old windows that can be installed anew.

LIGHTING

Bathroom lighting should be practical and flattering. There should be enough general light that the room is comfortable with the flick of a switch, but not so much that the user is surrounded by a glare that bounces fiercely off tiles and mirrors. This general light should be supplemented with fixtures placed to enhance specific tasks, such as shaving or applying makeup, reading, showering, and retrieving things from storage spaces. Lighting can be installed with dimmer switches so that the brightness can be adjusted as desired. Ideally, at least one of the fixtures should be controlled by a switch just inside the door so that guests and sleepy heads won't have to grope in the dark.

The specific look or styling of the fixtures can unify or destroy the mood and style you have worked to create, so it should be in keeping with them. There are many lighting fixtures designed specifically for bathroom installation, including some that incorporate exhaust fans or heat lamps, but virtually any fixture that meets your needs can be used. If your bathroom reflects the style of a particularly old house, you may find it difficult to find fixtures that are in keeping with the period and also give sufficient light; in that case unobtrusive recessed ceiling fixtures combined with decorative sconces may be the best compromise. If your bath is contem-

porary, there is no end to the variety of fixtures available, many of which have industrial or Oriental design origins. Look again at Chapter 1 of this part, "Style and Mood," for other lighting fixtures chosen with an eye to ambience.

Both general and task lighting can be provided by wall fixtures, ceiling fixtures, or a combination of the two. The medium-sized contemporary bath **at far left** has a raised ceiling, and two wall-mounted fixtures in the gable ends provide general light. Recessed fixtures in the soffit over the vanity light the mirror. The glow spilling through the doorways attests to additional fixtures that light the toilet and shower alcoves. The number and type of fixtures you select for your bathroom will depend upon the size and layout of the room; a very high or low ceiling may preclude the use of certain types. Additionally, the types of bulb and shade or glass play an important role; fluorescent bulbs tend to have a blue or cold cast, incandescent ones a red or warm glow that is kinder to the complexion. Translucent shades (including any molded glass that actually forms the fixture) will give a softer light than those that are transparent. Fixtures that are designed for bathroom use are usually equipped with or specify use of particular bulbs developed to provide nonglaring, flattering illumination.

175

Ceiling fixtures can be recessed, surface-mounted, or pendant. Recessed fixtures come in two sizes and use either spot or flood lamps. The spots concentrate the light into a small area, whereas flood lamps cast a larger circle for more general light. A row of the smaller recessed fixtures with smaller bulbs will create more even light and be less noticeable on the ceiling than the larger-sized ones. Surface-mounted fixtures need some sort of shade to diffuse the light. Track lighting systems offer great flexibility and a variety of bulb and shade types. Wall-mounted light fixtures can be track systems, multibulb strips, or individual lamps or sconces. Many surface-mounted fixtures can be used on either ceiling or wall with equal success. The directional focus of some recessed and all track lights can be adjusted.

If appropriate to the design of the room, combining a light source with a valance can be a successful way to provide illumination without the intrusion of fixtures. In the bath **below**, a

© Jessie Walker Associates

© image/dennis krukowski, Design:

valance running the length of the mirrored wall over the vanity masks fluorescent tubes. Because the ceiling slants up away from the wall, light is diffused both up and down so that task and general illumination are generated by one source. This valance is covered in the same paper as the walls, producing a tailored and unobtrusive effect. One drawback to this installation is that the lamps and back of the valance are reflected in the mirror, so the mechanics should be tidy.

Fixtures that light a mirror should extend to the front of the glass but be positioned to minimize reflected glare; if you are using a surface-mounted medicine cabinet, be sure that the light source is sufficiently in front of it. Multibulb strip lights such as those **above** are a common choice for mirror illumination. Inspired by theatrical makeup lights, they create a professional ambience. Strip lights are available in a variety of styles and module lengths. There are also fixtures that combine strip-mounted bulbs with a single light-diffusing cover, should you like this concept but object to the naked bulbs. Note the narrow ledge where the tiled dado turns to meet the mirror in this bath—a nice touch where there is no vanity counter—and the open recessed shelves next to each pedestal lavatory.

Industrial design has had a tremendous impact on the look of home furnishings in the twentieth century. As new materials and fabrications are perfected, products with technological origins are finding their way into contemporary homes. The pristine bath **below** is accented with strong black lines and chrome fittings.

The unusual light fixtures are integral with the mirrors. This is a clean, witty design; the arched mirror is reminiscent of a classic medicine cabinet, the arched chrome arms that support the lamps swivel to or from the glass, and the lamps themselves pivot in their mounts. Aimed upward, the light is bounced off the ceiling and walls rather than directly off the mirror.

If a bath is not intended for everyday grooming, you might decide to sacrifice function to form. In the powder room **above**, elegant brass sconces cast a gentle glow on a wonderful Louis XVI French mirror. This tiny room has a formal air, with marble wainscoting, subtly striped wallpaper, a tailored Roman shade, and a classic pedestal lavatory. Although the ambient light from the sconces is fine for a makeup check, it might be insufficient for a complete grooming routine.

FINISHING TOUCHES

Your new fixtures are in place, gleaming with carefully selected fittings; the tile is installed, the inlaid border as handsome as you had hoped; the vanity, wall sconces, window trim, and crown molding are perfection; and the wallpaper stripe is picking up the tile and trim colors nicely. Everything in the room is as envisioned, but somehow the effect feels a little bland, sterile, uninhabited. Have the mood and style you worked so hard to pull together eluded you after all? Probably not—it sounds as though your stage has been well set and is simply in need of dressing. The spaces in which we live and work take on their final character when we touch them with our own personal taste, and it is not until artwork, accessories, and personal effects are in place that we can truly claim ownership or feel at home. No matter how good the design of a room, it will not work until all the small pieces that impart character and make everyday use convenient and familiar are in place.

FINE-TUNING THE AMBIENCE

The accessories you choose for your bathroom will put the finishing touches on the decor, bringing the mood and style into focus. If they are well chosen, they will make the room unique, with the effect of the whole being greater than that of the sum of its parts. And choosing them should be fun, since the decisions will be based more on aesthetic than technical requirements. While accessories should be in keeping with the mood and style of the room, and even enhance it, they need not look as though they stepped off the coordinated pages of a manufacturer's catalog. When you put the finishing touches on a room's decor, you can allow a purple patch or two to find its way in, acknowledging the more eclectic parts of your personality. Since it is unlikely that many of the things you think you want to use will be custom made, you can test them in the space and return them if they are not successful. So open your eyes, trust your instincts, and be creative.

Mirrors; towel bars, hooks, and pegs; hanging shelves; soap dishes and the like; artwork; shower curtains, linens, and rugs; dressing table accoutrements; flower vases and potted plants; chairs, stools, magazine racks, and small tables; waste baskets; and even cabinet hardware may all be among the accessories needed to put the finishing touches on your bathroom. Depending upon the design and construction requirements of the room, you may not always be able to delay their selection until the rest of the room is complete; even if you must specify them early in the process, they will be important in putting the polish on your concept.

Successful decorating is not based upon a pretty arrangement of obviously coordinated elements—things don't have to match, they have to work on both a practical and an aesthetic level. If they are usable things, they should function properly as well as look appealing. If they are simply decorative, they should make a contribution, adding color, revealing character, hiding a defect, or filling an awkward space. In any case, they should be proportioned so as to look as though they belong in the space assigned to them, neither overwhelming nor being overwhelmed. When the room **below** was redone, the owners covered the walls with full-blown, old-fashioned roses and added

© image/dennis krukowski, Design:

© image/dennis krukowski, Design:

a countertop of a solid synthetic material reminiscent of white marble, both perfectly in keeping with the original period of the house. The countertop was cleverly shaped to provide access to the window; the narrow extension is a wonderful shelf for the collection of ornate silver pin and powder boxes, which picks up the silver-toned finish of the chrome shaving mirror, classic medicine cabinet, and porcelain lavatory controls. The still-life collage of paper and fabric on the wall is a personal touch, adding a bit of sentiment to the nostalgic ambience.

The older bathroom **above** was given a cosmetic face-lift that works well with its original appointments. There is an interesting introduction of color into the original all-white scheme: the smoky gold of the marble border; the pink and gold of the framed botanicals; the smoke, ecru, and pink of the taffeta lavatory skirt; the antique patina of the shelf brackets; and the urn of potpourri—all subtle and faded and right at home with the wonderful old frame-fronted medicine cabinet and classic fixtures. The new gold-and-porcelain fittings and the wall-hung rose vase awaken the mood with a touch of strong color. The mirror reveals lace drapery at the window, which, along with the French mats on the ribbon-mounted prints, the gold-rimmed white glass on the lavatory, the urn, and the sphinx, completes the air of formality.

Mirrors

The nostalgic elegance of the two previous baths is hardly appropriate for the sleek, clinical bathrooms of today's newer homes. Fortunately, industrial designers are introducing all sorts of products that are appropriate, and home furnishings stores and catalogs offer a wide selection of state-of-the-art accoutrements with sleek lines, slick finishes, and a clean demeanor. The chrome-armed mirror **at left** has a well-proportioned athletic stance that would be appropriate to a white-tiled room filled with glassed-in shower, whirlpool tub, and laminate cabinetry. The chrome-finished wheeled cupboard is a very contemporary alternative to a pine or wicker washstand.

Up-to-date need not mean high-tech. The swing-armed mirror **above** is classic, good looking, and suited to either a traditional or contemporary situation—variations on this theme can be seen in the diverse rooms in these pages. The swing arm is more elegant than the old-fashioned accordion-joint extension arm, and the glass itself swivels in its bracket. If you have a large stall shower, you might consider mounting one of these in it for one-stop shaving and showering.

Mirrors provide a true point of focus in a bathroom: you look into them for obvious reasons; they are more often than not situated so as to command attention; and they reflect the rest of the room, reiterating its mood, which makes their look doubly important. And you must consider not only the style of the mirror frame, but its size in relation to the wall and to the height of those who will be using it. There is no reason to limit your selection to ready-framed mirrors in home furnishings stores. Any picture framer can make a mirror for you. The variety of molding profiles and finishes is extensive; the prices are more reasonable than you might expect; and you are far more likely to find one that is interesting and appropriate to your room than if you limited your search to ready-made examples. Be aware that custom frames are sized by the dimensions of the rabbet that holds the glass, not by the perimeter of the molding; let your framer know that the dimensions you have measured are for the finished size of the frame, and he or she will know how to compensate for the

width of the molding you have chosen. Antique and thrift shops are also a good source of interesting frames. Beveled edges add elegance and authenticity to many period looks. If you wish to have them put on the glass, it can usually be done for a small extra cost.

The mirror in the elegant bath **at left** is in a formal frame with a black panel and burnished gilt edges. Look closely—that is indeed a reflection of the charming cord-sashed shower curtain, but the columns have no architectural reality; they are etched in the glass itself. While this one was done by a professional, you can achieve similar effects yourself. Most crafts-supply stores carry glass and mirror etching creams, which are applied through stencils and are very easy to use. If you are timid, you can practice on a small piece of mirror to see how the technique works.

Framing materials need not be limited to wood and metal in traditional profiles. Something less conventional may be more important to the mood of your room simply because it is unexpected and therefore commands more immediate attention. A

decorative mirror frame can take the place of other artwork. It can also acknowledge or accent the materials used for cabinetry or trim, continue a theme or motif found elsewhere in the decor, or even satisfy the yearning for a touch of pattern that you could not afford to indulge in the fixtures or tile. In a very small room it might be the one ornate, whimsical, or patterned element you rely upon to crystallize your vision; in a larger one it might unify or add diversity to the look. A painted ceramic frame like the one **on the right of page 182** can inject a touch of quiet elegance into a country decor and keep it from being too rustic. This frame is very pretty set against the ocher of the rough plaster wall and the polished wood counter, calling up visions of a country villa in Italy or Portugal. The same environment would be instantly transported to the American Southwest should the frame be fancifully punched Mexican tin. Other eclectic framing choices might be twigs, vine or everlasting floral wreaths, or shells or pebbles glued to a wood base. If you are skilled with your hands, you might like to create your own original design, or you could look in a crafts or ethnic or folk art gallery for something handmade.

Shelves, Towel Bars, and Practical Accessories

Bathrooms are like bedrooms and kitchens in that there is always a need for convenient places to put things: cosmetics and grooming aids, assorted towels, and, of course, the small decorative objects that give the room character. In many contemporary baths, the vanity offers counter space for jars, bottles, brushes, and flowers, and some incorporate towel bars. In traditional baths a shelf mounted next to or above the lavatory is sometimes all the counter space that can be accommodated. Home furnishings stores and catalogs offer a variety of small ready-made hanging shelves, many of classical or witty design, sometimes including bars or pegs for hand towels. A simple glass shelf mounted on brackets, like the one below the white frame-fronted medicine cabinet on page 180, or the column-

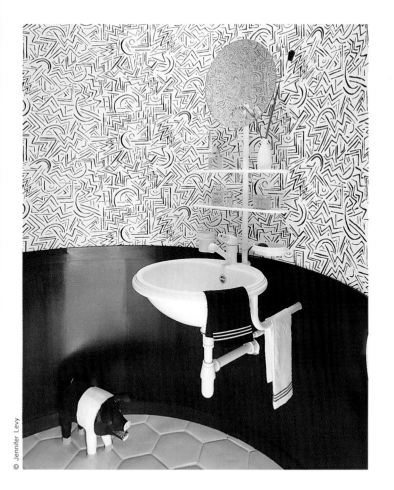

© Jennifer Levy

etched mirror on page 182, is almost always appropriate and can be made to any size. There are brackets for this purpose included in many towel bar lines, and most hardware stores offer a selection as well. Bed-and-bath shops and eclectic home furnishing stores often carry more unusual hanging shelves and brackets; faux finishes and wrought iron are currently popular. If your bath is very modern, there are also wire or plastic shelves available; these can vary in design from the streamlined to the witty. The new wall-mounted lavatory **on the previous page** has been fitted with a clever tree of shelves that includes glass and soap holders and is topped by a mirror. The combination of tubular and sheet plastic is perfect in this somewhat funky, somewhat retro, somewhat industrial setting. Note the tubular towel bar on the lavatory, an appropriate nod to the metal bars often attached to older wall-mounted models.

Towel bars are very often chosen to coordinate with fixture fittings or to pick up a color accent used in the tile or trim. They may be ceramic, wood or metal, or opaque or transparent plastic; they often combine two materials. In looking through these pages, you can see numerous good-looking and effectively chosen wall-mounted towel bars. If wall space is limited, you might consider a towel valet like the chrome-finished tubular one **at right**. These can be positioned by the tub, shower, or lavatory, or even in a guest bedroom to keep a shared bath clutter-free. Some wall-mounted tubular metal towel racks hide a wonderful secret: heat. This is almost a necessity in homes that lack good central heating, where a warm towel will soften the blow felt stepping out of a hot bath into a chilly room; they are also a good idea in humid climates, where damp towels can mildew. The towel bar chosen for the pretty attic bath **on the left of page 185** has a polished brass finish, as do the tub accessories, the lavatory fittings, and the sconces. This is a lovely, summery country room, cool and a bit romantic in blue and white. The fluted lavatory, garland border, and formal accessories are on the dressy side, but not so much that they are out of place with the rough-timbered eaves or the pine-topped vanity.

Courtesy of Chambers

There are a number of easily overlooked small practical accessories without which a bathroom cannot function smoothly, and which may or may not be built in: toilet paper dispenser, toothbrush and glass holder, soap dishes, shampoo shelves or baskets. Soap dishes and shampoo shelves are included in molded tub and shower surrounds; soap dishes, toothbrush holders, and toilet paper dispensers are included in some lines of wall tile (as are towel-rod brackets). Selecting these pieces to coordinate with tile or fixtures will assure them a smooth and unobstrusive role. If this is not possible, or if the look is not what you have in mind, then home furnishings, hardware, and bed-and-bath shops and catalogs all offer a number of alternatives that range from classic to ultramodern in design, and may be wood, metal, ceramic, molded plastic, or even enameled cast iron. Unless you are putting together a truly eclectic room with lots of antique or funky accents, you will probably be happiest if you choose these small necessities to be of a type, particularly if they are to be permanently attached to the walls.

The puzzle of where to put grooming aids is particularly marked in old-fashioned bathrooms—one reason they are so often furnished with small tables and large baskets. Freestanding tubs look marvelous and are usually comfortable and relaxing to recline in, but they lack the convenience of flat surrounds

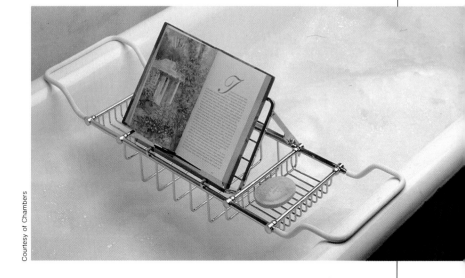

Courtesy of Chambers

and the molded soap dishes or shampoo ledges found in built-in models. To compensate for these practical shortcomings, use some of the metal baskets designed to rest on or hook over the tub edge. These may be all-wire or wire with perforated sheet-metal bowls, but they come in various configurations to hold soaps, shampoos, and grooming aids; the one **above** incorporates a book stand, essential to a leisurely soak.

Curtains, Rugs, and Linens

Textiles bring softness to the mood of a room. In a bath, it is likely that the only chances you have to use this softness will be at the window, on the shower, on the floor, and with the towels; in some contemporary baths, towels are the only textiles, which helps to explain why these rooms tend to have a hard or cold feeling. One great thing about bathroom textiles is that they are not built in, so they are easy to change. And changing them can sometimes do wonders to lighten, brighten, or add sophistication to an existing decor.

The way a bathroom window is dressed has as much to do with the need for privacy as it does with mood and style.

© William B. Seitz

Opaque or stained glass, blinds or shutters, and draperies or curtains are all options. Whichever you choose, the look of your window treatment can be, but is not necessarily, a finishing touch; it is likely to be integral with the wall covering. Window treatments are shown and discussed throughout this book. That being said, if you have decided not to use curtains or draperies that coordinate closely with your wallcovering, you do have the option of changing or adding a window treatment at any time.

In traditional baths, the room is usually protected from water by a shower curtain rather than doors. Shower curtains can match or complement the window curtains or the wallpaper; this can give the room a neat, pulled-together look or it can be boring or overwhelming if it gives the impression of too much of a good thing. If there is no window treatment to coordinate with, or if repeating it would be overwhelming, then consider the effects that different textiles are likely to have upon the mood of the room and select something that will enhance it. Do you feel the need for pattern? For color? For texture? Should the curtain be translucent so it does not block light? Is the room formal or informal? Should you add some sort of trim to the curtain? Do you want something whimsical, feminine, tailored, or silly? Virtually any fabric can be used as a shower curtain (though some, silk and velvet, for instance, are not terribly practical) as long as you protect it with a plastic liner. Bath and home shops also stock a variety of ready-made shower curtains in prints and solids, some of which coordinate with rugs or towels.

The quiet gold tones accenting the spacious bathroom **at left** provide it with an aura of understated elegance. The room is uncluttered, but each accoutrement—the marble lavatory, old-fashioned brass fittings, inviting claw-footed tub, fringed damask lampshade, bold scrolling leaf border, and even the pastoral nude—has an element of grandeur. Each holds a place of considerable importance in the overall design, which is at once formal and romantic. The gilt feet and stenciling on the tub help to dress up a fixture that could seem heavy against the rather delicate wallpaper motif and slender table legs. The lovely sheer

curtain hanging in the tub is appropriately elegant, but more importantly it brings a touch of intimacy and privacy to the open room. Consider using window sheers, a cutwork tablecloth, or a pretty white bed sheet for a curtain such as this; if the curtain is more ornamental than practical, you could use antique lace.

Bath linens make a room feel habitable and welcoming. They can be chosen for color or style, injecting a bright, dressy, country, or funky note, or even betoken the season. Your everyday

linens should, of course, be absorbent, sturdy, and infinitely washable; those in a powder room, or displayed as ornament, can be less practical. Antique stores are a wonderful source for old romantic white linens, and new ones imported from the Orient are readily available. The brass rack **on the previous page** holds a mix of new and old fancies flushed out with plain white terry cloth, a great way to make a collection look more lavish. This is just one possible array; your bath might call for a lineup of tattersall tea towels, tartan and paisley napkins, or just plain terry cloth in jewellike colors. And if you like to do needlework, plain linens look wonderful with hand-stitched trims.

Bathroom rugs should be selected with an eye to practicality if they are likely to get wet—or you should provide a bath mat to protect them when bathing is in process. Bathroom rugs can bring color and pattern to a plain floor, and can muffle sound and protect bare feet from cold tiles. Because of the inevitable dampness and heavy traffic, any rug you put in the bathroom should be washable or easy to vacuum and air out, but you are certainly not limited to the once-ubiquitous chenille. There are rag rugs in endless colors and patterns, braided rugs, printed rugs, straw mats, and floor cloths. If one suits your decor and makes the room more comfortable, use it.

PULLING IT ALL TOGETHER

As you assemble your finishing touches, stand back, take a look at the effect, and assess its success. Do you have all the things you need to make the room comfortably usable? Mirrors? Towel bars? Shelf, counter, or tabletop space? Linens? Curtains? Are they arranged conveniently? Are they arranged attractively? Is the effect too busy, too coordinated, or dull? Do you need a splash of color or a touch of the unexpected? Is there empty space or a jarring element? Have you put too much in a room that should be less adorned?

When a room is finished, it will tell you who it is; it will be in character, with all its disparate elements working together. The turn-of-the-century bath **at right** is very self-assured in spite of its numerous and rather eclectic contents. What may at first appear to be a serendipitous collection was quite carefully assembled around the basic decor: black-and-white floor; white fixtures and wainscoting; red-and-white stylized floral wallpaper; dark-framed mirror-front medicine cabinets. The arrangement is balanced and orderly, with the three mirrors, the three glass shelves, and the two lavatories flanking the wicker stand. The accessories were chosen to balance the weights and colors built into the room by carrying your eye from one area to another. The red-and-white hand towels and striped curtain are a counterpoint to the wallpaper; the white lamp shades give a nod to the fixtures; and the extravagant folding screen and pedestal dressing stand balance the heavy mirror frames and keep them from jarring. There are lovely small touches here, too: the glass pulls on the mirrored doors, the chrome fittings and shelf brackets, the wonderful old shaving mirror, the dressy sconces, the potted plant, the crystal pitcher and glass. The folding screen with its sinuous Arts and Crafts fabric is certainly that purple patch, the element of surprise, but its lyre shape works with the floral sprays on the wall, and the red trim around each panel is a perfect finishing touch.

This room may be far from your ideal bath, but it works with great aplomb, and much can be learned from it. Remember the mood and style you set out to create. Do you have a room that you want to use first thing in the morning and last thing at night? If not, add, subtract, or change accessories until your room works comfortably for you.

PLANNING A BATHROOM

Whether you are designing your own bathroom or working with an architect, interior designer, or designer-contractor, in order to plan the specifics you must coordinate four interdependent sets of criteria: the desired mood and style, the material options, the type and frequency of use to which the room will be put, and the space available. Up to now, we have concentrated on developing a mood and style and enhancing it through selection of potential fixtures, floor and wallcoverings, lighting, and accessories. Once you have the idea of what you want your bathroom to look like, you are nearly ready to prepare a final design. But before you do so, stop to ask yourself how you really plan to use the room.

WHAT HAPPENS IN YOUR BATHROOM?

Obviously, bathrooms take care of certain basic sanitary needs, and for some people pure function is all that is required. But a bathroom can also be a place to relax, to socialize, to exercise, to dress, to do the laundry, or to bathe the baby. Sit down and make a list of things you expect the bath to accommodate. As you make a final plan, ask yourself if you have made provisions for all of them; if you have not, can you do so? If it is not possible, are you compromising wisely? Here are some basic issues to consider; add your own as they occur to you.

• *What kind of bathroom is it: master, household, child's, guest's, half-bath, powder room?* The type of bathroom may dictate the number or grandeur of fixtures; the mood and style of the decor; and the amount of everyday storage necessary for towels, toothbrushes, robes, etc.

• *How many people will use this bath? Is it the only bath in the house?* A bath with only one user can be as personal as desired; one that is shared must accommodate various needs. If there is only one bathroom for the household, consider putting the toilet in a separate room to ease traffic in the morning and evening; ideally there should be a lavatory with it.

• *Will there be more than one person in the room at one time?* If so, what concessions need to be made to privacy? Should the toilet be in a cubicle or an alcove? Is a two-basin vanity called for? Is extra floor space needed for dressing or grooming? Should there be a comfortable place for nonbathers to sit for conversation or reading aloud? Will you be assisting small children in the bath or with brushing their teeth?

• *Do any of the users have special needs? Are they elderly or handicapped? Are they very tall or very short?* Bathrooms for wheelchair users have special door, floor space, and fixture requirements, and the elderly rely more on hand grips and railings than the young. Even if these are not issues of particular concern to you, some concessions to them may be a wise investment, particularly if you plan to resell your home in the not-too-distant future.

It is easy to overlook needs dictated by varying human proportions, but there is nothing more disconcerting to a tall person than a shower aimed at his shoulders or a mirror that reflects only his collarbone; conversely, a shorter person may have trouble adjusting the spray on an out-of-reach shower head or need a step stool to use a lofty looking glass. Larger people will be more comfortable in larger tubs. And the safest way to get into a tub is to sit on the edge and swivel into it; this can be difficult if the tub is too low.

• *What is the attitude of the users to time spent in this room — brisk and utilitarian or prolonged and relaxed?* Be sure that lighting is adequate for all activities planned. Allow for audio or television equipment if desired. Plan ahead for bookshelves or magazine racks. If potted greenery is part of your dream decor, check that the light is sufficient, and consider if you need an extra sink for watering or want to build in a greenhouse window.

• *What activities other than the obvious will be pursued in this room?* Do you require space for exercising? Do you want to be able to sit for any of your grooming routine? Will the room double as a laundry and require a folding table or ironing board? Do you want to plan ahead for a neat way to drip-dry hand-washed items? Do you need a changing table for an infant, with diaper storage nearby? Don't overlook the necessary electrical outlets for equipment for these activities.

THE SITUATION

There are technical considerations and building code regulations that must be met before a bathroom plan is finalized. Professional designers and licensed contractors will be familiar with these; if you are evolving your plan alone, be sure to check with the local building inspector and get the advice of plumbing, building, and electrical contractors to ensure that your plan is feasible and legal.

The location of a bathroom within the home affects the ease and pleasure of its use. If there is only one bath, it should be near the bedrooms and accessible from a hallway. If there is a master bath, the door to it should be within the master bedroom. For reasons of privacy, bathrooms should not open directly onto living or dining areas. Building regulations generally preclude them from opening onto kitchens. If you are concerned about the resale value of your home, a full bath on the ground floor is always an enhancement. Although you may be tempted to sneak an illegal or not-to-code bath into your home, you might find that potential future owners will not be able to get a certificate of occupancy for it, making resale impossible.

If it is convenient, rooms with plumbing should be situated near to one another. This allows the primary water supply and drain to be shared and minimizes costly runs of pipe. It is not necessary for all fixtures to be on the same wall.

Bathrooms should be as soundproof as possible. Cupboards, closets, and bookcases on common walls can muffle noise, and doors should not be flimsy. If your bath shares a wall with a living area or several bedrooms, consider using special soundproofing wallboard or insulation to enhance privacy. The whir of an exhaust fan will mask the sound of running water; some fans are automatically activated when the light is turned on. However, this white noise may itself be unpleasant, and therefore, a fan that is separate from the overhead light may be desirable. Exposed pipes should be boxed whenever feasible to mask the sound of water traveling from one floor to another.

Bathrooms should also be well ventilated. This not only mini- mizes damage from condensing steam, it eliminates odor. Win- dows and operable skylights are great assets in warm weather, however an exhaust fan should be provided for cold-weather use or interior rooms. If you live in a particularly humid climate, consider adding an outdoor shower, screened for privacy as necessary. There is no better way to protect your decor from steam and mildew damage, and the sun and moon and fresh breeze give new meaning to cleansing the soul.

Because water conducts electricity, most building codes include strict electrical regulations; depending on the area of the world in which you live, these may apply to outlets, fixtures, and switches. Be sure that you understand the requirements. Outlets and wall switches come in a limited variety of styles and finishes, something to remember as you site them, as they can be an obtrusive and unwelcome finishing touch—especially when multiplied by mirror images.

THE FLOOR PLAN

Bathroom floor plans do not have to follow particular rules; bath- room activities are not governed by work triangles (logical traffic patterns) the way those of the kitchen are. Within the limitations of the space available, the fixtures can be arranged however you desire. Smaller baths are frequently arranged so all the plumb- ing is on one wall, with the length of the tub across a perpendic- ular wall or with the tub along one wall opposite to the toilet and lavatory. If the room is a bit larger, you may have the option of placing the fixtures along three or even four walls, and in any situation the placement of doors and windows will influence the final plan. The mid-size bath shown **at upper and lower right** has a triple-window dormer with fixtures placed under the eaves at each side. The tub and shower stall are on one wall; the two- basin counter is on the opposite wall; and the toilet is on the wall opposite the windows. The door to the room is next to the counter. Note how thoughtfully this room was planned: there are

storage niches under the eaves by the tub and counter; there is a seat built into the shower; the hip bath is under the eaves where standing might be difficult for taller people; and the spacious shower enclosure is transparent so that it does not intrude upon the room. The mirrored wall bounces the natural and artificial light into the tub and shower, and the reflection makes the room appear bigger than it is.

The configuration of the particular room will often suggest an arrangement; an L-shape, a long, narrow space, a pitched ceiling, or a dormer alcove can each be used in a different and creative way. If you are adding or enlarging a bath, you may be able to borrow space for one or more fixtures from an adjacent room. You might even find room under the stairs for a half-bath, like the rustic one **below**, where the vanity is topped by an old stone trough. Although the tendency today is to make the bath-

room spacious, you should refer to your checklist to see if you really need and want a big room—you might get more use from that expanse between tub and vanity if it were housing your home office in the bedroom.

An easy way to visualize potential floor plans is to draw the dimensions of the room to scale on graph paper, marking the doors and windows, and then cut out "fixtures" drawn to the same scale, which you can move about on the paper outline. Some rule-of-thumb dimensions follow. Clear floor space should be adequate for you to rise, bend, and turn; steps to a tub or room for a door to swing may require more space.

• Toilets are 19 to 21 inches (48–53cm) wide and 27 to 31 inches (68–78cm) front to back; they should be centered in a space 24 to 44 inches (60–110cm) wide with 18 to 36 inches (45–90cm) between the front edge and the opposite wall or fixture.

• Bidets are 14 inches (35cm) wide and 25 to 27 inches (63–68cm) front to back; they should be centered in a space 24 to 44 inches (60–110cm) wide with 18 to 36 inches (45–90cm) between the front edge and the opposite wall or fixture. They should be placed next to and in line with the toilet.

• Lavatories are 18 to 30 inches (45–75cm) wide and 16 to 21 inches (40–53cm) front to back; they should be centered in a space 28 to 44 inches (70–110cm) wide, or set at least 2 inches (5cm) from an adjacent fixture, with 18 inches (45cm) between the front edge and the opposite wall or fixture. (For vanities, standard cabinet depth is 24 inches [60cm]; you must allow space for the doors to swing open.)

• Stall showers are 32 to 36 inches (80–90cm) wide and 34 to 36 inches (85–90cm) from front to back; they should be set at least 2 inches (5cm) from an adjacent fixture with 18 to 34 inches (45–85cm) from the front edge to the opposite wall or fixture. If there is a door, be sure to allow space for it to swing open.

• Tubs are 30 to 40 inches (75–100cm) wide and 60 to 72 inches (150–180cm) long; they should be set 2 to 8 inches (5–20cm) from adjacent fixtures with 18 to 30 inches (45–75cm) between the side of entry and an opposite fixture, 20 to 34 inches (50–85cm) between the side of entry and an opposite wall. The controls should not be blocked by an adjacent fixture.

If space in your bathroom is not terribly tight, then you have the freedom to develop a less conventional floor plan. Perhaps you can plan a self-contained shower room, like the ones shown on pages 149, 170, and 171. Perhaps you would like to incorporate some level changes from one area to another, with steps up to a tub or dressing area. You might wish to add columns or an archway to define and separate the space.

Courtesy of Laura Ashley

© image/dennis krukowski, Design:

If the room is small and there is no way to make it larger, consider facing one section of a wall with mirror, which will give the illusion of additional space. When the small turn-of-the-century bath **at left** was renovated, one tall, narrow wall was mirrored above the wainscoting; when you look into it, you believe momentarily that you are seeing another room with matching windows beyond a half-wall. This is true trompe l'oeil, and the mirror is a happy blend of contemporary detail with traditional architecture.

You might want to place the tub away from the walls; this is a luxurious touch, acknowledging that there is more space than necessary so you need not feel hemmed in as you soak. The old-fashioned bath on the left of page 173 and the contemporary one on page 174 have the tub positioned centrally. You can even set it perpendicular to a wall, as in the chintz-curtained boudoir **above**, which invites visions of intimacy.

If you are planning new wall construction, whether a completely new house or an addition, or an extensive renovation or a conversion of an open space such as a loft or barn, don't automatically design your bathroom within the confines of a box. Building alcoves for some of the fixtures rather than arranging them on the open floor between four walls can create privacy and add visual interest. It may also be a wiser overall use of space, as the alcoves can be tucked next to closets or other alcoves in the adjacent rooms.

The house **shown on these two pages** has an open, rather Oriental feeling, and the interior spaces are defined with unique partitions rather than conventional walls. The sliding

© Jennifer Levy

door on the translucently glazed partition in this master bedroom leads to a cleverly designed bathroom. There is a tub to the right, a recessed shower stall set into an alcove opposite the door, and a two-basin vanity on the wall opposite the tub. The toilet is immediately to the left of the sliding door in another alcove that projects into the bedroom—enclosed by the interesting angled partition with the horizontal niche—and another sliding door separates it from the main part of the bathroom. The translucent glazing allows light from the skylight and clerestory window to filter from the bath into the adjacent room. In the bathroom, the walls, floor, and shower and tub surround are tiled, and the wall over the vanity is mirrored above and below the high window. On each side of the shower, beautifully partitioned cabinets hold towels, toiletries, small sculptures, and a television. The vanity front is recessed to hold additional towel bars. In terms of open floor space, this bathroom is not very large, but with its all-white, glass, and mirrored decor, sliding door, cathedral ceiling, and views of the sky, it feels quite spacious.

While this house is unusual at first glance, the thinking that went into the development of the bath can be transposed to many situations. After all, each home is unique to the people who dwell in it and expect it to provide them with their own idea of comfort. As you develop the plans for your own bathroom and look at the many ideas found in this book and in your file of clippings, make note of the things that really catch your attention—whether they be whole concepts or small details—and analyze their attraction for you. Is it because you like the way they look or the way they work or both? Measure them against your checklist for function and practicality, discard those that are not feasible or appropriate, and then think creatively about how to incorporate those that are truly right for you. Keep editing your ideas until they come together in a cohesive plan and don't be afraid to ask for professional help. When you are happy with the design, then go ahead with the execution; you'll be able to pamper yourself in the finished room before you know it.

197

p a r t   f o u r

CLOSETS AND STORAGE

INTRODUCTION

A PLACE FOR EVERYTHING AND EVERYTHING IN ITS PLACE

Everyone has possessions. Most of us have more than we know what to do with. Age has nothing to do with accumulation—even newborns have requisite accoutrements: diapers, powder, towels, and many changes of clothing a day. Children have books, toys, homework, clothes. Teens possess all of these things plus music. The rest of us have not only all the necessities of work and play, but also homes, cars, and gardens that require cleaning and maintenance. And, of course, we must provide food at least for ourselves and very likely for family and friends. Hobbies, sports, collectibles? Think tools, equipment, supplies, books, magazines. The potential for clutter lurks in every life. If you let it grip yours, your possessions may be rendered useless—chances are you'll not be able to find them when you need them.

There are people who thrive on chaos, and who love the thrill of the chase, the hunt for the known but misplaced sock, the recipe buried somewhere in that pile of clippings, or the screws that must have fallen behind the workbench. But for most of us, life is too short to be devoted to these frustrations. Unfortunately, the more we own the more daunting the task of imposing order on our possessions is, and most of us live with more objects than space in which to put them.

Inanimate objects don't organize themselves. Few of us have household help, genies, or the good mice of fairy tales to scurry about whisking clutter out of sight. And even if we did, there would have to be a place to put it all. The first step to conquering clutter is to identify it, the second is to find a place to put it, and the third is to organize that space efficiently. Once you admit that the task must be done, you'll find that imposing order is neither difficult nor boring; if you go about it creatively it can even be something of a game in which the challenge is to find the perfect way to store everything. The reward is that you'll enjoy easy access to it all.

Look around your home and identify the source of the clutter problem. What kinds of possessions are out of order? Look also for general solutions. What kinds of storage space are available already and what kinds could be added? Is the problem that your home lacks storage space or that you are not using what you have wisely? Are you planning a new home or addition? If so, analyze your present storage system and be sure the new space will provide you with as much storage as necessary.

This book is organized in three sections to help you to develop a general storage concept and then refine its details: storage areas, such as closets and utility rooms; storage units, such as bookcases and cupboards; and storage accessories, the organizational aids that fit into these spaces and make it easy for you to maximize their potential. There are certainly many cluttered situations that might require help from a carpenter, but today there are innumerable ready-made storage units and devices available from home stores and catalogs; these products have a diversity of function that can solve many problems and complement many styles of decor. So roll up your sleeves—there has never been a better time to get organized.

201

STORAGE AREAS

Wouldn't it be wonderful if every home and apartment was designed with dozens of closets, a pantry, a laundry, a home-maintenance workroom, and an extra room in which to pursue whatever job or hobby the occupant fancies? Then indeed there could be a place for everything, everything in its place. Such dwellings would have to be palatial if they included regular living space as well as all that storage, and few of us can afford such grand quarters.

Most homes do include some of these features, and with a little thought they can be modified to include those they lack. The storage areas we have can be organized to new levels of efficiency or even adapted to new uses. With the right poles and shelves, a closet can hold a lot of clothing; with shelves and no poles, it can be transformed into an office or workshop. Hallways can become pantries, and corners can be furnished and organized to be the extra space you so desire.

Maximizing storage space is easier in some homes than in others. The task is, of course, less complex if you are beginning with poorly organized storage areas than if you have to create a space to organize—any closet is better than no closet, as anyone who lives in an old, closetless house can attest. However, if you have defined the type of storage you need, there is a good chance that a careful appraisal of your home's layout will provide you with the space to devote to it.

CLOSETS

The word "closet" generally refers to a small room or compartment whose floor and ceiling are on the same level as, or just a step above or below, the adjacent room, and which can be closed off from that room in some manner—a closet is a space that is closed in. Indeed, one of the attractions of a closet is that it conceals whatever it holds, and too many of us tend to just toss things we don't know what to do with behind the closet doors. In new homes closets are usually recessed in a wall, while in older ones they are often boxed out into a room, but this can depend upon the location of the closet and the layout of the home. We think of clothes closets, china closets, linen closets, broom closets. We sometimes use the word disparagingly: "the bedrooms were no bigger than closets" or "I could never cook in that kitchen, it's just a closet." Today we also think of converted closets, those that are adapted for less conventional use. In a studio apartment the kitchen appliances might be built into a closet. A home office can also be concealed in a closet.

Most of us feel that closets can never be too numerous or too large, but many of us fail to really organize the closet space we have. Whatever the end use of your closet, you will fit more into it and get the most out of it if you design the interior to accommodate the specific items to be stored. The manner in which you do this can be as simple or as elaborate as whim or budget dictates: you can have shelves and cabinets custom-built or use one of the modular systems from home stores or catalogs. Most of the beauty of a well-organized closet lies in the order revealed when the doors are opened. If the interior structure is gorgeous as well, so much the better, but beautiful shelving in the wrong configuration won't help you to locate your socks.

If you need to create a storage area where none exists, consider building a closet along one wall of a room. Although you will lose some open floor, you will gain a well-defined and contained space. Even if you have to give up some pieces of furniture—a chest of drawers or a table—you can compensate for their loss by building alternate units into the closet.

Clothes Closets

Clothing is something we all have to store. We have clothes for work, for play, and for evenings out. And most of us have different wardrobes for different seasons as well. There are clothes that should be stored on hangers and clothes that should lie flat; there are small articles that seem to store themselves in heaps and tangles; and there are shoes, bags, and hats that shouldn't be crushed and therefore take up precious space.

With all the closet-organizing systems available today, there is no reason to limit your storage to a single pole hanging at shoulder height with one deep shelf above it and shoes claiming valuable floor space. The large closet **at left** has been filled with storage modules that preclude any future mess. This closet is shared by two people, and the interior space has been divided to accommodate their different types of clothing. To set up a system like this, first sort your clothing by category and size, putting all like elements together, then allocate the space necessary to store each type. A glance at this closet shows that if it were spanned by just one pole, there would not even be enough space for the hanging clothing it now holds, and any additional items would no doubt be stashed awkwardly on the floor. Shorter poles installed at varying heights accommodate clothing efficiently and free up additional space for drawers and shelves. Assorted shelf and drawer depths provide space for a maximum number of shoes and folded garments and assure that they will be easy to find and put away. Although large and deep drawers might hold a lot, they do not make efficient storage for smaller items, which are easily jumbled together. Take

the time to measure folded clothes to see how much space is needed for each type, then try to provide storage units that will hold them compactly without useless leftover space. Choosing adjustable shelves will give you greater flexibility, particularly if you rearrange your wardrobe with the changing seasons. If your closet has a high ceiling, hang several shelves one above the other, positioning them to hold short stacks of blankets or folded clothing or numerous rows of hats and bags; towering piles are difficult to keep balanced, particularly when you want the item on the bottom, and have a tendency to tumble down on your head.

Different types of in-closet storage units provide different kinds of protection for your clothes. Things that you wear frequently should be fine in open compartments behind the closet doors. Fragile or infrequently worn garments may need additional protection. This closet was fitted with a number of enclosed storage units, which protect contents from dust and can be fortified with moth repellents or sweetened with pomanders. Transparent doors and bins keep the contents visible, so you know at a glance what is where—and when it begins to get messy.

Conventional closets can easily be retro-fitted to be made efficient. Today there is such a variety of modular storage units available that anyone should be able to find and set up a system such as this one with little or no help from a carpenter. However, if you prefer your closet system to have the status of fine cabinetry, and have the skills or budget to have storage units custom-built, you can apply the same organizational principles to your wardrobe and then refine the efficient-use-of-space concept to exactly fit your needs.

The large walk-in closet **on page 206** uses beautiful, well-planned cabinetry to provide the ultimate in efficient wardrobe storage. The owner's extensive wardrobe was sorted and analyzed by type, quantity, and size, and storage was cleverly designed to make the most efficient use of the available space and keep the contents accessible at a glance. All like items are grouped together so wardrobe options are clear, and dressing

If you want to protect your linen closet from insect pests, consider lining it with aromatic cedar or using cedar pomanders in tightly fitted drawers. Dried herbs such as lavender or tansy are also believed to discourage nibbling insects, and they impart a wonderful lingering fragrance.

Bar/Liquor Closets

If you do a lot of entertaining, or if a cocktail hour is part of your domestic routine, you might want to store liquor and glassware in a living area where they are easily accessible. A recessed

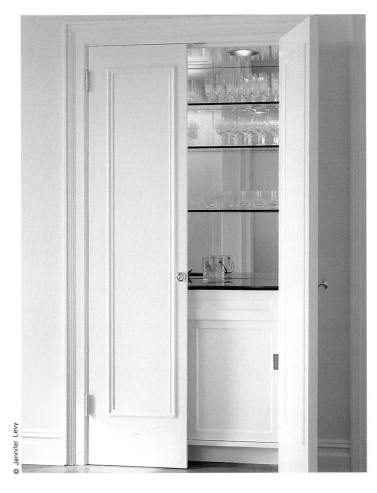

closet is much more convenient, spacious, and stable than a wheeled cart; close the doors when not in use and it will assume the architectural demeanor of the remainder of the room. Doors that lock will deter small children and secure the bar when you are away from home.

The small closet **at left** is just the right size to hold glassware and fixings. A set-up such as this one would be easy to arrange in any closet; just be sure that the first shelf is far enough above the counter to permit movement of arms, bottles, and glasses. The glass-and-mirror interior not only sparkles, but is also easy to wipe clean. Sliding doors on the cabinet don't interfere with the bartender's knees.

If you have room for a walk-in closet, it can be arranged even more effectively. The one **above** has been fitted as an elegant

209

wet bar with a small sink and an under-counter refrigerator. The white-flecked marble counter, dark blue paint, and sparkling glassware are all reflected like a starry night sky in the mirrored walls. Because the doors to this closet open inward, they are not hazardous to people or furniture in the adjacent room.

Media Center and Library Closets

A closet can be the ideal location for a media center. Closed doors will protect equipment from traffic and dust, and also hide it from view, which might appeal to those who find the look of audiovisual components incompatible with their decor. In the

contemporary room **at left,** modular shelf units fit right into a closet to house tapes and components, with drawers on one side providing additional storage. Architecturally, this closet is untrimmed, and when the doors are closed it goes without notice. Most closets—unlike bookcases—are deep enough to hold a television; if you wish to include one, be sure that it will be convenient for viewing when installed, or place it on a rolling cart. If space in the room is tight, consider putting bifold doors on the closet for more convenient access.

Although most book lovers have a desire to display their libraries, sometimes there is just not space enough for bookcases. Closets can be converted to diminutive libraries very easily, as the addition of simple shelves and an overhead light is all that is required. The tiny closet in the dining room **at left** holds a surprising amount of reading material. When closed, the door is flush with the wall and nearly fades from view, making a clean background for the columned entry to the next room; a conventional bookcase would have been distracting in this location. This idea of carving a closet into an otherwise useless bit of wall could be adapted in a variety of ways and is a good one to remember when confronted with an awkward floor plan, as is sometimes unavoidable in a renovation. A small library like this one could be a great addition if its contents were dedicated to the room that held it—what cook would not love a space like this for cookbooks in the kitchen, what gardener would not be thrilled with gardening books in a sun room? Of course a larger or more conventional closet is equally suitable for book storage. If you are turning a spare bedroom into a home office or study, you could set up the clothes closet there as a dust-free library with much less trouble than would be involved in building attractive bookcases, and no floorspace would be lost.

Office and Workspace Closets

Today more and more people are trying to find space for work or study in their homes. Those who do not have extra rooms often try to establish a workspace by setting up a desk or computer station in the bedroom with some hanging shelves along one of the walls. The major disadvantage to this set-up is that it is impossible to put your work away; if it is not out of sight, putting it out of mind can be difficult. One way to create an office in a limited space is to dedicate a wall to it and box a shallow closet out into the room, as was done very attractively in the bedroom **on page 212**. Actually a series of bookcase-depth alcoves, this closet is simple, effective, and very good-looking. Each bay can be closed with a conventional miniblind, so no floor space is lost to the path of doors. And because the dark

green frame matches the window trim, it looks as though there is a wall of windows on that side of the room when all the blinds are down. Each of the bays is fitted with storage shelves. The large bay with its hanging shelf, bulletin board, and desk top serves as a workstation for the jewelry designer who lives here; a folding chair can be collapsed and tucked away when the blind is lowered. If this worktable were modified with a drop-leaf tabletop, it would provide a larger surface that could still be hidden when not actually in use.

A closet can also provide officelike space for a school-age child, establishing a private and professional environment for homework and creative projects. The one **on the left of page 213** has plenty of bookshelves, a bulletin board, and an ample-sized desk. The closet doors were removed for this conversion, but their presence is a matter of individual preference. Although it is used by a grade-schooler now, this study space is appointed well enough to support an increasingly heavy work load as the child grows. In fact, an adult could work quite comfortably here.

If you are setting up an office in a closet, be sure to make allowances for proper lighting fixtures and electrical outlets. You might want to install low-glare fluorescent lights under the shelves or recessed lamps in the ceiling. A strip of outlets along the back of the counter would accommodate an electric typewriter or a computer and printer, desk lamp, calculator, and any other necessary equipment; a phone jack nearby would be necessary to hook up a phone and answering machine, modem, or fax. If you are planning the workstation for a growing child, consider making the height of the desk adjustable so that it can be raised as he or she grows. If you are planning to use a computer in a space like this, consider installing a slide-out under-counter tray for the keyboard. These prevent wrist fatigue and free up desk space. There are also many ready-made computer workstations that could be used alongside a smaller built-in desk or set of file drawers.

If you do not suffer from claustrophobia, consider setting up an office space in a walk-in closet. These have the obvious

211

© Jennifer Levy

accomplished. Depending upon the location of your closet, it might be possible to add a skylight to bring in light and air, and lend an illusion of space.

If the idea of a closet office appeals to you but your existing closets are full, consider transferring the contents to alternative storage furniture, perhaps an armoire, blanket chest, or bureau. You may find that this overall use of space is both efficient and attractive, as the office paraphernalia will be concealed when not in use and storage furniture can be very handsome.

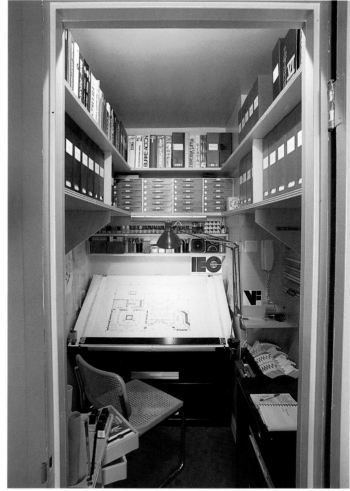

advantage of a greater expanse of wall on which to hang book-shelves, bulletin boards, or pegboards. The compact office **at right** has been very neatly slotted into a small space, but it holds everything the owner needs to pursue his trade. The simply constructed shelves are exactly proportioned to hold various binders and art supplies. Next to the snugly fitting drafting table is a small level shelf that can hold a mug out of elbow's way. The artist's taboret in the foreground provides additional compact storage with swing-out drawers. A set-up with as little floor space as this one presupposes that the occupant will be sitting still when using it, but that is, after all, how most office work is

213

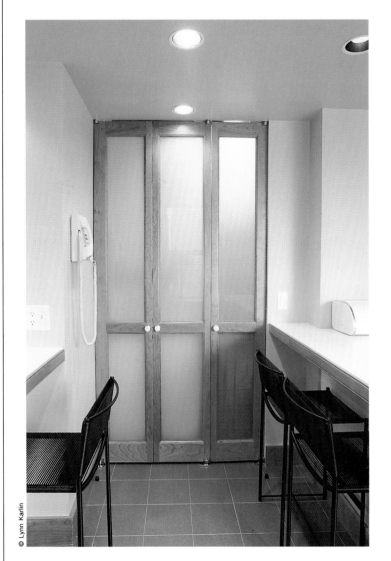

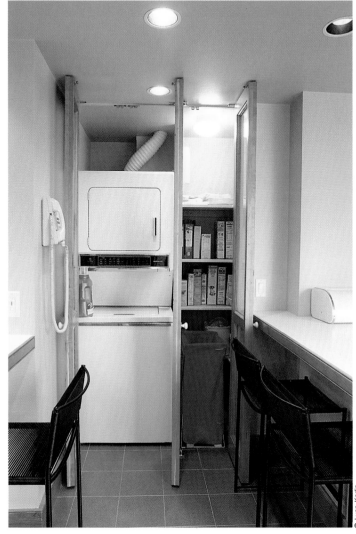

Laundry Closets

If you live in a small house or apartment that does not have a basement or utility area for a washer and dryer, you can hide a compact and perfectly functional laundry in a closet. It is easiest to do this in a kitchen or bathroom where there are already plumbing supply and waste lines, or in a room or hall adjacent to these. If you like to line-dry your clothing, try to locate the laun-

dry as close as possible to the back door so you won't have to carry heavy wet clothes any farther than necessary. The disadvantage to putting a laundry in a closet is that there is not usually room for a folding table, but the advantage is that the closed doors hide the appliances and supplies and muffle operating noise. While the kitchen is not the ideal place to handle clean clothes, it is more convenient than the local laundromat; if locating your laundry appliances in the kitchen is your only option, try to place them away from the cooking or eating areas.

The kitchen closet **on page 214** was designed specifically to house a tiny laundry and storage area. The three narrow doors are handsome and use a minimum of floor space when open. One pair opens to reveal the appliances, while the third door gives access to shelves and a rolling hamper. A stacking

washer/dryer such as this one takes up the floor space of only one appliance and is ideal for closet installation.

If you have the room, conventional side-by-side appliances can be hidden behind closet doors as well, and you can mount shelves on the walls above them. One end of the bathroom **at lower left** is devoted to a laundry center, with a utility sink, plenty of shelving, and a washer and dryer. All the shelves are shallow so that you won't knock your head when scrubbing at the sink or loading the washer; those over the machines are high enough to allow the lid of the washer to open. The space under the sink stores larger cleaning supplies. The bifold doors provide ample access but don't take up much room when ajar. Stacking laundry units may also be installed side by side. Since they are both front-loading, a countertop can be installed on top and used as a folding table.

DRESSING ROOMS

There is something marvelously luxurious about the idea of a dressing room, conjuring up visions of the eighteenth-century boudoir, replete with recamier, lace, and ruffles—or leather, boot polish, and tweeds in a gentleman's cabinet. If we have the space for them, dressing rooms can be private places for dreaming, reading, and letter writing (or long phone conversations), the place where we assemble our thoughts as well as our appearance. You can set up a dressing room in a small room, alcove, or passageway near bath or bedroom; it can be lined with closets or arranged inside a very large one.

The way you will use a dressing area and the space available will ultimately determine how you organize it. Should it be designed for straightforward utility—storage and dressing—or for relaxation as well? Will it be private or shared with a mate? Will visitors pass through it, or will it be truly sequestered? If it is open to other rooms, you will probably want your dressing area to continue or complement their decor; if it is self-contained you might want to establish an entirely different style.

more contemporary or less "feminine" mood, you can adapt the concept to suit your taste.

You might prefer to set up a dressing area so that all your wardrobe options are in full view, or you might not have the budget for built-in cupboards. The informal dressing room **below** is decorated with the contents of the owner's eclectic wardrobe; the effect, if a bit chaotic, is rather fun and certainly personal. There is nothing complicated or expensive about setting up a space like this one. The shelving is rudimentary; the

The pretty, garland-trimmed dressing area **above** is a passageway between master bedroom and bath. It is lined with closets and other built-in storage, and a mirror set into the alcove above the bureau is convenient for attending to hair and makeup. Additional counter space opposite the double closet doors provides a surface on which to assemble an outfit. The proportions of this room are too tight to allow for a chair, but the elegant bathroom beyond is spacious enough for a comfortable one. This is a serene environment in which to pamper yourself. Of course, the raised panel cabinetry, stenciled decoration, and lovely overhead lampshade are all cosmetic touches that do not affect the way this space works as a dressing area; if you prefer something with a

© Bill Rothschild, Design: Dorothy Diamond

216

© Bill Rothschild

into a dressing area by adding shelves and hanging poles. When the broken-up space **at left** was allocated as a dressing area, the short runs of wall actually prompted an organizational plan. Each section is put to good use and fitted with easy-to-size and readily available closet gear. The stacked plastic boxes in simple cubbies are an inexpensive alternative to a complex custom-made cabinet, and the adjustable shelves and clothes racks are mounted on brackets screwed to the walls. A sunlit dressing space like this one could invite you to linger if furnished with a comfortable chair. Or if you set up the ironing board here, your pressing and mending might seem less of a chore. One word of caution—things stored opposite a window should be shielded from sun damage with some sort of opaque material, or the shades should be drawn when the room is not occupied.

PANTRIES

Depending upon how they are set up, pantries can store comestibles, cleaning supplies, paper goods, table linens, pots and pans, dishes, or all of the above. Before modern supermarkets and the family car made food shopping convenient, homemakers purchased staples in bulk (or harvested and preserved them) and stored them as best they could without refrigeration. Large families or large homes with servants required lots of kitchen gear as well as eatables, and it was once common to find a food pantry adjacent to the kitchen, and perhaps a butler's pantry between cooking and dining areas. During this century, as family size dwindled and living space shrank accordingly, the pantry was sacrificed to make way for more important things—like bathrooms. Today, anyone who has a large family, entertains frequently, or simply loves to cook probably longs for more copious kitchen storage space. And even if none of the above applies to you, smart shopping suggests buying in bulk when things go on sale; if you have nowhere to stash all the bargains, you can't take advantage of them.

clothes hang on a portable rack; the wall is faced with gingham-covered corkboard; and the furniture, like much of the clothing, came from the local thrift shop. But it's a great space, full of dreams and memories. Again, you can adapt this concept to reflect your own taste; the whimsical contents of this room give it character, but they are not what make it functional.

Sometimes a home will have awkward spaces, perhaps wrapped around a stairwell or created by an altered floor plan. Should you have such a space near a bedroom, you can turn it

Pantries can be self-contained rooms, with or without doors, or they can be set up in shelf-filled closets or in hallways or passages. They can be lined with cupboards or open shelves, although cupboards with doors will, of course, keep things dust-free and out of view. Larger pantries often include counter space for unpacking groceries or resting dishes between shelf and table. A pantry with a sink can double as an extra clean-up

or food-preparation space or be used for flower arranging. Some people prefer to put the refrigerator or freezer in the pantry to free up space in the kitchen, but this is convenient only if the rooms are adjacent.

The simple pantry **at left** is just an alcove in a shed tacked to the back of an informal summer house. The walls are lined with open shelves; one side is devoted to tableware, the other to food and paper staples and a few linens. The shelves are not so deep that things could get lost on them, and one run of boards was omitted on the lower left to accommodate taller items. You could easily create a similar storage system with freestanding

© Lynn Karlin

© Bill Rothschild

standard wire or metal industrial shelves, which have the advantage of being adjustable.

The passageway in the circa 1920 Colonial Revival home **at left** is a true pantry built for gracious living. There is plenty of cupboard and drawer space for storage, and counters for serving or unpacking. The old icebox at the center of the righthand wall is not really functional today but is good for short-term use. Note that the glass-paned upper cabinet doors, which are quite large, slide rather than swing open—a good idea where floor space is limited. Half-curtains shirred on rods conceal some of the interiors so there is no pressure to arrange essential but not-so-attractive staples. This room has been thoughtfully decorated in an English Country mode and is very pretty, but it would be a pantry to envy whatever its decor.

To take best advantage of a pantry, decide if you wish to use it for everyday items or for long-term storage of things infrequently used. If your pantry supplements a very small kitchen, you will probably put things in it that you use all the time and you will want to set it up so that they are readily available. If it offers you extra storage space, then put things in it that you don't need every day: the lobster steamer, large stock pot, baking pans. If you buy in bulk, or preserve your own jam, use the pantry for back-up supplies and keep only the open jars or packages in the kitchen proper.

If you already have a pantry, arrange the things you want to keep in it by type and size; supplement the existing cabinetry with stacking wire or plastic shelves and bins to make it more functional. If you are building a pantry, gather the items you wish to store, or samples of them, sort them by size and type, and then plan the shelves to hold them conveniently. Put larger items in deep drawers and shelves, and smaller things in shallow ones so that you won't have to hunt to find the item you want. Don't plan to stack heavy items above shoulder height—falling cans can inflict nasty wounds. If you are compulsively organized, make arrangements for inventory lists to be posted inside cupboard doors so you can keep an accurate account of what you use. Those who rent out their homes during vacation seasons might want an inventory posted to help tenants find what they need and to provide a checklist for themselves.

UTILITY SPACES

Workspace and supplies for basic home maintenance—chores like laundry and ironing, and pastimes like flower arranging, quilting, or model building—are often relegated to the basement, garage, or back entryway, where, depending upon the individual situation, they might be alloted a small corner or a generous area. Whether or not these spaces are finished and decorated like the rest of your home probably depends upon your taste and budget, and often has little to do with how functional they are.

When planning a utility area, define its use, measure the space available, and make a list of the things that need to go into it. Is it a laundry room, a mudroom, a potting shed, a workspace for hobbies, a place to store sports equipment? Analyze the kinds of equipment and storage you will need: shelves, cabinets, appliances, pegboards, worktable. If you are interested in concealing small equipment and supplies, or storing awkward things like bicycles or lawn chairs, check out home furnishings catalogs and visit a home center and cabinet showroom to learn about the many ready-made and do-it-yourself storage options available. If you are pursuing a particular craft or hobby, look through magazines devoted to it for workspace ideas. Your first reaction when you make your list might be one of panic, but you will find that someone is making a storage device for almost everything imaginable.

To help you visualize a plan, draw the space to scale on graph paper, then draw any furniture, appliances, or cabinetry to the same scale on another piece of paper and cut them out. Move the cutouts around on the space plan to determine an arrangement that will accommodate them and leave you as much wall space as you think you will need for shelving, pegboards, or other hanging storage. Be sure to include adequate lighting fix-

219

tures in your plan; if the utility space is really just for storage, you will need enough general light to be able to find things easily, but if it is also a work space you will need good task lighting over work areas. You will also need appropriate electrical outlets, plumbing, and vents for appliances and other equipment.

Laundries and Housekeeping Centers

Laundries are probably the most common utility spaces in today's homes. They very often accommodate more than just the basic washer, dryer, and folding table, and include an ironing station, sewing area, and sometimes storage for housekeeping equipment such as vacuum cleaner, mop, and broom. The way you set up yours will depend upon its location in your home, the space available, and the tasks you wish to do in it. If the laundry area is in an unfinished basement you might not want to sort, mend, or iron there; if it is not near the kitchen it might not be the ideal place for a broom and mop cupboard.

At the very least, a laundry should include the washer and dryer and storage for detergent and other laundry supplies. Ideally there will be floor space for sorting soiled laundry if not a counter or table for folding clean clothes. A nearby utility sink is helpful for hand-washing delicate items, removing stains, rinsing hands, and measuring detergents. Everything but folding can be done in the no-frills laundry center **at right**. This utility room has a stall shower alcove for washing mud and sand from beachgoers' and gardeners' feet; with a pole recessed inside, it provides a perfect spot to hang wet clothing and keep the drips off the floor. If you don't have space for a full-length shower, consider replacing the cabinet over the sink with the kind of wire shelving that has a hanging rod attached. In fact, if your laundry area is very small, you might prefer wire shelves to cupboards, choosing to sacrifice closed cabinet storage for their lighter, airier look and easier access.

If you use front-loading machines, you can build a counter on top of them for folding clothes. The washer and dryer **on the**

© Jessie Walker Associates

left of page 221 were installed with a counter above and bifold doors in front; when these are closed the appliances are completely hidden. The cabinet located in front of them holds tilt-out hampers for color-sorted soiled laundry.

The laundry/housekeeping center **on the right of page 221** is located at one end of a large kitchen. The appliances are on opposite sides of a small hallway, and a door across it muffles their noise when they are in use. The wall of cabinets acts as a pantry and a center for ironing, cleaning, and entertainment. The ironing board is full-sized and folds into the drawer in which it rests (boards like this one, and others that fold down out of

shallow wall cupboards, are available from a variety of sources).
The drawer underneath holds items waiting for the iron's touch;
you could put a large, deep basket into the dead space above
this drawer if it was needed. There is an electrical outlet inside
the cabinet for the iron and the television. The wire racks in the
cabinet on the left are a slide-out pantry unit; these come in
assorted sizes and could be used to hold the small gear necessary for any number of pursuits instead of the grocery staples
for which they are primarily intended.

Garage or Workshop Storage Areas

Storage in an unfinished area such as a garage can be plain
and simple as long as it is sturdy. Inexpensive, ready-to-
assemble utility shelving such as that **on page 222** can be configured to hold a variety of tools and gear. This set-up holds
assorted storage bins that have hand-hold cutouts, which make
them easy to move about, a large storage crate that rolls into the
shelf system on casters, and a small pegboard that keeps hand
tools visible and organized. A conventional, hinged-drawer
metal toolbox keeps small tools and parts organized, clean, and

Courtesy of Inter IKEA Systems B.V.

portable. Large metal utility hooks screwed directly into the walls are good for hanging bulky or awkward items such as garden hoses or heavy-duty extension cords; if you mount them in pairs, they can hold ladders, bicycles, or folded lawn furniture.

There is nothing elegant about this set-up; it is a raw space, and there is no need to worry about spoiling it with rough usage.

If you plan to use an area such as this for work as well as storage, be sure to set it up with adequate ventilation and good general and task lighting, as well as lots of electrical outlets so that you will not be tripping over long cords. If the floor is hard and unfinished, install a fatigue mat in front of the workbench to prevent back and leg strain.

Summer Kitchens and Flower-Arranging Areas

The summer kitchen—a room to clean and store freshly harvested produce—was once standard in many homes. Few people build them anymore, but if you do have one it might be an ideal spot for flower-arranging or caring for potted plants. Even if you don't happen to have such a room, you could create a space for these or similar activities in a mudroom, garage, basement, or corner of a large kitchen or bathroom. All you really need is an easy-to-clean and water-resistant area with a sink, counter, good light, and storage space for vases, pots, and supplies.

The pretty work area **at right** has a sink in a stainless steel counter with a high backsplash and is blessed with lots of natural light. The faucet is wall-mounted and fairly high so that buckets and vases can go right into the sink to be filled; a hose attachment or sprayer would ensure that particularly tall vessels could be filled. A small chest of drawers holds floral supplies and tools. Simple shelves hold vases and crockery; the narrow one over the sink is just deep enough to hold small jars with additional supplies. Cup hooks screwed into the underside of the wider shelf are perfect for bunches of drying flowers; you could also hang ribbons or coils of wire from them while you were working. The space under the counter is open for easy access when hands are messy, and the wire bins roll out when needed. If you like to make wreaths, consider putting some hooks into the wall to hold them vertical while you arrange them. If you want to set up a room like this one to care for houseplants or bonsai, you might consider adding a pegboard to the wall for small and frequently used tools like pruners and trowels. If you were really going to use the room like a summer kitchen, you would probably want a larger or double sink and lots of hanging baskets so washed produce could drip-dry. Some window-covering system for filtering bright daylight, like the miniblinds used here, will help to keep fresh flowers and produce from wilting.

© Bill Rothschild

STORAGE UNITS

No matter how spacious or charming a storage area is, it must be fitted with racks, shelves, and cupboards before it can work efficiently. And certainly many of our storage needs have nothing to do with closet space, but with the integration of small everyday items within our general living areas. We may or may not be as concerned with putting things out of sight as with putting them out of the way in an orderly— and perhaps attractive—manner. We have books, audio equipment, tapes and CDs, and all manner of collectibles as well as clothing, kitchen necessities, leisure-time gear, and home-office paraphernalia. Very few of us want to wade around piles of stuff, so we look for ways to organize it, get it off the floor or table, keep it safe, and sometimes display it; to do all of this we rely upon various storage units.

In deciding how to organize and store your possessions, the first thing you must do is categorize them and choose a potential storage location. This will probably be self-evident: kitchen things go into the kitchen or a pantry; tableware might go in the kitchen, pantry, or dining area; clothing in a bedroom or dressing room; hobby supplies wherever you plan to work with them. Books and collectibles, however, might be appropriately housed in almost any room or even in a hallway, and you should ask yourself whether you are more interested in storing or displaying them when deciding upon a location.

Once you know what you wish to store and where you want to put it, you must decide whether the storage is to be concealed or in plain view and whether or not you want it to be decorative as well as functional. If your storage is out in the open— cabinetry, bookcases and other shelving, and freestanding furniture—you probably want it to be the best-looking you can afford, as it will be part of your home's decor. If it is to be concealed in a closet or small room, you might or might not be concerned with the aesthetics as long as the system you have chosen offers sturdy and efficient storage.

You must next decide whether your storage units should be built-in or freestanding and whether they are to be custom-made or assembled from stock units or ready-made furnishings. The options are as diverse as your ideas and will no doubt be guided by the particular situation, the desired aesthetics, and your budget. One of the best ways to conceptualize a storage system that will work for you is to do a lot of research: look through home-decorating books, magazines, and catalogs and make a clipping file of good ideas (photocopy anything you don't want to cut up).

As you look for ideas, it is very important to keep an open mind and learn to distinguish a clever concept or a good use of space from a merely attractive or beautiful design. A good idea can be interpreted in any number of decorative styles, so don't worry about whether something is wood or metal, painted or stained, elaborately trimmed or simple and sleek when you are looking for ways to utilize space. Once you have decided what sort of system you want and what configuration it should have, then decide upon the aesthetics and look through your file again for stylish inspirations. If your concept is well-planned *and* beautiful to look at, it will be doubly successful and a great asset.

BUILT-INS

Built-in storage—pieces firmly attached to walls, floors, ceilings —becomes part of your dwelling place and so should be in keeping with the architectural style of your home. (Shelves without casings may be firmly attached to the wall but are not considered true built-ins; they are discussed on page 238.) Before deciding that you must have something truly custom built, look through home-furnishings catalogs and visit furnishing stores and cabinet showrooms; most large building supply vendors offer stock cabinet units with more styling and finishing options than you might have realized.

Bookcases

There is perhaps nothing more evocative of sophisticated living than a wall of elegant built-in bookcases. No matter what the architectural style, the fact that someone cares enough about books to create a permanent library space for them conveys a sense of intellectual curiosity and contemplation; a room with well-filled bookcases invites relaxation and good conversation.

Most bookcases project about thirteen inches (33cm) from the wall. They can be shallower and still accommodate many sizes of books, but if they are much deeper the space is likely to be wasted on anything but art books or records. If the shelves are adjustable, you will have more flexibility in filling them since you will be able to group volumes of like size. However, if you wish to arrange your library alphabetically, you might do better with fixed spacing tall enough for most volumes, supplemented with a section for oversized ones. When planning the height for bookshelves, don't forget to include the thickness of the shelf itself as well as the height of the books; you cannot put two rows of ten-inch (25cm) tall books in a twenty-inch (50cm) high space.

If one room of your house is devoted to quiet activities—a library, den, or study—consider lining one or more walls with floor-to-ceiling bookcases. Those in the library **below** are very elegant; the gleam of the polished oak casework and paneled doors and wall combines with the formal furnishings to make this

© Phillip H. Ennis

is trimmed with a simple molding at the top, and the lower section at the far end is enclosed with pairs of molding-trimmed doors.

Bookcases set into a wall can appear lighter and less bulky than those built out from one, and can be a good choice for a small room that might be overwhelmed by a lot of casework. Depending upon the situation with which you begin, they may also be less expensive to construct. The simple inset bookcases that flank the marble fireplace **on the left of page 228** provide ample storage but do not intrude too much into the room, which, while comfortably cozy, could not carry all of its furniture along with elaborate bookcases. If you have a wall that is interrupted by some sort of architectural projection—a chimney or boxed service pipes, for instance—you can build a wall surface flush with the projection and cut a bookcase, or another sort of cupboard, into it. You could also build a false wall about a foot (0.3m) away from a partition wall (between two rooms) and set bookcases into it from both sides, much as you might add adjacent closets opening to each side of a shared wall.

room a classic and inviting retreat. The small, softly lit alcove where the sofa sits among the books is a wonderful, intimate touch.

The craftsman-built storage wall **above** is much more contemporary, and while not as grand, is very good-looking. The shelves are permanently fixed at regular intervals and there is ample room for books; the case also displays assorted works of art, which are handsomely framed by the figured hardwood that lines the back. The case sits on cupboards that provide concealed storage, making it suitable for a home office as well as a living room.

A wall in a hallway or other space that is too small to furnish and too large to be only a passageway is an ideal location for a bookcase. The one that runs along the wall of the foyer/living room/dining area **at right** is fairly shallow, but it holds thousands of volumes as well as some favorite artwork. It stops short of the high ceiling to showcase additional pieces, for book storage at that awkward height would be inconvenient. The design and construction of this bookcase are about as uncomplicated as is possible; the adjustable shelves are flush with the plain casing, which

© Daniel Eifert. Design: Kate Altman

© Jennifer Levy

The boxed beams, cornice, and raised-panel cabinetry in the living room **below** are reminiscent of Early American architecture, but the turntable, tapes, tape deck, and speakers would certainly mystify anyone living at the time this style originated. Sliding shelves and drawers make everything accessible as needed, but when the doors are closed, most of the twentieth century is hid-

Entertainment Centers

Audiovisual equipment can be very frustrating to store. It takes up a fair amount of space, requires all sorts of electrical connections, must be easily accessible, and is generally contemporary and slick in design. If you have an old house or favor period-style decor, you might not want an intrusive expanse of black lacquer and shiny chrome. Even if your decor is industrial, you probably want to group your media systems and install them in a protective environment where they will be safe from knocks and jostling. You can buy freestanding entertainment-center cabinets in various period styles; these are usually designed to look like armoires and can look great if they work well in the space you have available. You can also put shelving in a closet, as seen on page 210, which might be an ideal situation if the space is conveniently situated for viewing or other access. There is also quite a variety of pull-out, swivel, and lift-up shelving hardware that enables virtually any type of cabinetry to be adapted for media equipment. If you have room for a built-in entertainment center, you can design one that is functional and appropriate to your decor.

© Jennifer Levy

An entertainment center need not be in cabinetry per se, but—if appropriate to the style of your home—can be set right into the wall. The living room **below** has a mixture of traditional and contemporary architectural details with furnishings that are very modern. An interior partition forms a media wall, with a separate niche carefully cut for each piece of equipment. Two additional niches showcase decorative objects. One feature that makes this system aesthetically successful is the coordinated styling of all the equipment; if the pieces had different finishes it would not be nearly as pleasing. A drawback to a set-up like this one is that it is totally customized, and should any of the equipment need to be replaced, there could be problems of fit or visual harmony. And there is no way to conceal any of the components, which might be a drawback for some tastes.

© Bill Rothschild

den from view. If you are planning a system similar to this one, be sure that the *interior* dimensions of the drawers (or the spaces between the dividers) are increments of the tapes or CDs you wish to store—there is nothing as useless as space for half a tape. If you are storing LPs, the shelving must be deep and tall enough to hold them; most bookshelves are too shallow.

The bay next to an interior chimney wall can offer a convenient space for an entertainment center, as your furniture is most likely already focused toward the fireplace. The owners of the contemporary home **above** had a simple but very handsome Shaker-style cabinet built to house their media equipment. This system was very well-conceived, with pull-out shelving and a section of the counter vented and hinged to provide access to the turntable below.

Kitchen Cupboards

Most of us would find it difficult to say whether we store a greater number of items in the bedroom or the kitchen, and unless we have an uncontrollable passion for shoes or mixing bowls, it is probably a toss-up. The majority of all kitchen storage is built in, and the look of the cupboards—painted or stained wood, glass-paned or plain doors, stone or synthetic surface, plain or elaborate casework—has a tremendous impact on the overall look of

the room. Important as these aesthetic considerations are, it is the amount and convenience of kitchen storage that is crucial to the workings of the room, almost as crucial as having good appliances, and much more difficult to replace. Of course, other types of kitchen storage can be very effective and are mentioned in other sections of this book: pegboards, pot racks, wall-mounted shelves, and freestanding pieces such as dressers, étagères, or pie safes, which can all be functional and attractive.

Configuring Your Cabinetry Kitchen cabinets fall into four basic types: under-counter, over-counter, over-appliance, and whole-wall (tall). Under-counter cabinets are usually 2 feet (0.6m) deep and can include drawer and/or shelf storage. Over-counter cabinets are 12 inches (30cm) deep so that you won't bang your head into them when working or lose things in the back; they generally provide only shelf storage. Over-appliance and whole-wall cabinets can be the same depth as either of the other types, depending on where they are installed and how you plan to use them. Under-counter cabinets can be configured as islands or installed against a wall; over-counter cabinets can be hung from the ceiling over an island or against a wall. Whole-wall cabinets can be closetlike, with one door length covering the full height, or made up of several vertically stacked sections.

The amount of cabinetry you can build into your kitchen will be determined to a great extent by the size of the room and the general floor plan you have worked out. Somehow, possessions always expand to fill any available space, and it is not likely that you could provide too much storage, so take advantage of whatever space you have. The cabinet configuration used most often is a combination of over-counter and under-counter units; these allow for the maximum amount of counter space and work with the greatest flexibility around appliances. An expanse of whole-wall cupboards will make the room feel smaller, so they should be used where there is really a need or extra space for them. Over-appliance cabinets can be used as needed.

The state-of-the-art white kitchen **at left** is timeless and efficient in its appeal. It is light, well-appointed, easy to work in, and has plenty of storage space. The under-counter cabinetry is a combination of drawers and cupboards, ideal for storing cooking gear, utensils, and linens. Over-counter cabinets on the wall store crockery and staples. An over-appliance cabinet the depth of the counter tops the ovens, integrating them smoothly into the room; the cornice molding at the top is a graceful finishing touch that turns into a charming display ledge on the right-hand wall.

The shallow shelves over the cooktop keep spices and baking supplies handy; set up like this they are decorative, but if the assortment were less homogeneous, the effect might not be as pleasing—a problem with using storage that is open. Note that the under-counter cabinetry on the rear left wall is the same depth as the cabinets above it. This arrangement makes the counter space less useful as a work surface, but provides lots of storage while using a little less floor space, a potentially crucial factor when working out a kitchen plan. Because the room has high ceilings, a row of shallow over-appliance cabinets tops the glass-fronted cupboards, providing more storage for items that are used infrequently.

Inevitably, cabinetry will make a room seem smaller. Deep cabinets set adjacent to a window will also block sunlight, intensifying the feeling of diminished size by making the room darker. To minimize this effect, the over-counter cabinets in the kitchen **on page 231** are stepped away from the window, growing deeper and longer as they move into the room. The glass-paned doors and white painted woodwork make them seem even less intrusive, and the overall effect is quite charming.

Making the Interiors Accessible

The fact that a kitchen has an ample supply of cupboards does not ensure that it is well fitted with usable storage space. Too often the cabinets are fitted with poorly proportioned shelving or are so deep that

things get lost in the back. There is no need for this, as there is an abundance of hardware that allows shelves to slide out, lift up, or swivel. If you plan ahead, many stock cabinet shops can customize cupboard interiors to fit your needs, and a good carpenter can retro-fit existing ones.

Sometimes all you need to do is provide convenient access to cabinet interiors. Doors mounted on both exposed sides of the corner cabinet **at left** make it easy to put things in and take things out of this deep but narrow space. With this kind of access, nothing is too hard to reach, and heavy pans can be guided into place with a hand placed through each door. A frequently used but frustrating kitchen configuration finds countertops turning corners, with the large and valuable storage space underneath rendered virtually inaccessible. If there are cabinets on either side of the corner, you can install a revolving shelf unit that pivots out from the upright at the turn (like three quarters of a pie spinning on its center). The kitchen **at left** has a dishwasher on the right arm of the turn, and the adjacent cabinet is very cleverly fitted so as not to waste the space behind it. A

swing-out shelf—just one quarter of a pie—pivots out to lie flush against the drawers to the left, giving access to hidden drawers that slide out from behind the far side of the dishwasher. There is no need to force the upper half of your body inside the cabinet to try to fish out something stored in the back corner, and no danger of banging your head.

Cabinet shelves are often spaced to accommodate staples or tall glassware, and dishes or linens must be stacked to fill them efficiently. There is nothing wrong with stacking flat items, but if the stacks are too tall, it can be awkward to remove things from the bottom. In addition, if your glassware is not tall, the space above it is wasted. On the other hand, if the spacing between shelves is too tight, you can't get your hands inside to retrieve things at the back. A solution to this problem is to install a flight of pull-out shelves or shallow drawers, as in the cabinet **at left**. These ensure easy access to the back, keep stacked items manageable, and work as well for cups and short tumblers as for plates. Pull-out shelves can be fitted with dividers to store flatware, spices, or other small items. Be aware that the shelves themselves take up space, so plan carefully, and use quality hardware so that everything slides smoothly.

Wine Racks

There are any number of ready-made wine racks that can be purchased and inserted into a cabinet. However, if you are interested in establishing a more substantial wine-storage system, it is not difficult and can be quite attractive. One very simple option is to fit pull-out shelves with wooden collars that secure the bottles' necks, like those **at the upper left-hand corner of page 234**. One great advantage to this system is that the labels are easily read; however, if you regularly stock a large number of bottles, you might not feel this is the most compact way to store them. If that is the case, consider using a cubbyhole rack that coordinates with the rest of your cabinetry. The one **at the upper right-hand corner of page 234** fills the wall between the countertop and an upper cabinet, with its white

© Jennifer Levy

grid design complementing the multipaned cabinet doors. There is a small refrigerator set under the counter to keep additional bottles chilled. A cubbyhole storage system can take any rectilinear exterior configuration—tall and narrow, square, wide and short—depending upon your needs, so one can often be added to a space that seems otherwise useless. For easiest access, the cubbyholes should not be much deeper than the height of a standard bottle; they can be oriented parallel to the floor or set diagonally on their corners (though the triangular spaces at the edges of a diagonal system will be useless).

If you are into serious wine collecting, take a hint from vendors and restaurants to set up a truly efficient storage system. **At right**, a rack of oversized cubbyholes set diagonally holds many bottles, and a commercial refrigerator equipped with an inner cubbyhole rack chills many more. Contact a restaurant supply or industrial shelving vendor for other commercial storage options; a local retailer or vineyard can probably supply you with sources if your telephone book is not helpful.

Adjustable Shelving

Any kind of storage unit that has shelves can have adjustable ones, though you must generally plan ahead for them. The shelves in cabinets, built-in bookcases, and freestanding furniture, as well as those mounted directly on the wall, can all be designed to be moved to whatever level accommodates the items to be stored. Adjustable shelves often sit on metal brackets that hook into standards (metal tracks with lots of small holes), which can be surface-mounted or recessed. The brackets can either turn up at the end to cup the front edge of the shelf, or be flat so that the shelf can extend beyond them—which is generally more attractive. If the shelves are supported from the ends, rather than the back, they can sit on small pin supports, which are less obvious than brackets. Pin supports are designed to work with standards or to fit into holes drilled directly into the shelf carcass. Sometimes shelves simply sit on small strips of wood nailed to the walls and shelf carcass, but these are adjustable only in the sense that they can be added or removed at fixed intervals.

When planning adjustable shelves, don't forget to include the thickness of the shelf itself in your calculations; metal standards offer quite a bit of flexibility but the holes drilled for pin supports do not. The smaller the space where you are installing the shelves (as in a spice or medicine cabinet), the more important it is to plan ahead, or you might end up with extra useless space above the bottles or jars. Even when installing standards, if the vertical space is particularly tight it might be a good idea to take the time to figure out where to cut them (on or between holes) so that the brackets will sit at appropriate intervals. And don't forget that the holes in all standards along the same wall must be aligned or the shelves will not sit level.

SHELVES

Shelving is without a doubt the easiest kind of storage to add to any space. It can be fixed or adjustable, freestanding or wall-mounted. It can be amply proportioned to house oversized art books or just deep enough to hold plates or pictures leaned against the wall. Hundreds of styles of ready-made shelving are available, and simple, good-looking shelving can be custom-made by anyone reasonably skilled with hammer, saw, and paintbrush. Shelving materials range from wood, glass, stone slabs, and plastic laminates to wire, metal, plastic, and molded solid synthetics; very often two or more of these types can be combined. A nearly infinite variety of looks can be achieved, complementing any decor at a range of budgetary levels.

As you decide upon a shelving style that is appropriate for your situation, consider how you will use it. Is your primary goal to provide storage, and if so, how much and for what, or is it to enhance a room with an interesting piece of furniture that will provide a place to display smaller objects? Is function the most important thing, or a combination of form and function? Should the shelves be at fixed or adjustable levels?

Freestanding Shelves

Freestanding shelves should fit into your decor like any other piece of furniture. They can be extremely plain or elaborately detailed, as suits your needs, and because they can move with you from one home to another, can be a good investment. Before you make your purchase, be sure you know what you want to put onto the shelves and make sure that they are spacious enough, proportioned correctly, and as sturdily built as you need—not all freestanding shelving is balanced well enough to stand away from a wall. Some styles of freestanding shelves are modular or plain-edged so that you can easily place several units together, while others have moldings or detailed styling that makes them more appropriate to stand alone.

Courtesy of Hold Everything

against an empty wall or be used to enhance a closet system; some of these are designed to stack as well as butt together. The best models have adjustable shelves so that you can easily customize them to your needs. The tall, narrow modular units **at left** come in white and a variety of bright colors, which would be fun in a pantry, bath, child's room, workspace, or playroom— or perfect to place in a closet. Though narrow, these units are a convenient width for storing all sorts of things, and the adjustable shelves let you arrange contents efficiently.

If you need bookshelves and don't want to get involved with built-in bookcases, unfinished furniture stores are a good source of basic styles in a variety of sizes; you can stain, wax, paint, or stencil them as you wish. Thrift stores often have wood bookshelves just waiting to be refinished, and antique stores are a good place to look for more elegant ones, such as library cases with glass-paned doors.

Home centers and catalogs are good sources of inexpensive freestanding shelving, particularly modular units that can stand

not be adjustable. Although it is quite sturdy, industrial shelving looks lightweight and does not detract from the visual sense of space in a room, so it can be an ideal choice for a small or dark area. One obvious drawback is that small things might tip over or fall through the wires, so it is most suitable for storing large or flat-bottomed objects. In this contemporary living room, a three-tier unit serves as a plant stand and liquor cabinet, creating an effect that is casual but not unsophisticated.

Etagères and whatnots are light, open, freestanding shelves that are usually intended to display bric-a-brac. They are generally decorative in themselves and can be quite elaborate, sometimes including a mirror or an enclosed base cabinet. Although often considered fussy and old-ladyish, they need not be. Today there is a real vogue for using baker's racks—which are one kind of étagère—for kitchen or dining room storage and display. Baker's racks generally have some sort of worked metal structure with wire shelves for cooling fresh-baked loaves; these are sometimes covered with wood, glass, or marble. The one **below**, made of enameled wrought iron with brass trim, makes

Adjustable metal utility shelving, such as that **at left**, is also easy to find and inexpensive. It comes in several sizes, qualities, and finishes. Although sold knocked-down, it can be assembled easily by a single person. Utility shelving is perfect for garage or basement use, and here it turns a blank wall into a pantry. Utility shelving is sometimes a bit flimsy; it will gain stability when filled but might not be a good choice if active children will be playing nearby.

In the right environment, metal shelving can be decorative as well as functional. The industrial shelving **above**, formed of heavy wire, is available from office-, hospital-, and restaurant-supply vendors, and sometimes from home stores and catalogs. It comes in a variety of sizes and qualities and may or may

a very pretty substitute for a sideboard. A piece like this one would be at home almost anywhere in a summer house, and could be used to hold linens, plants, books, or crockery. Baker's racks come in any number of sizes and shapes. Old ones can be very expensive, but new ones are available in a range of prices in home stores and catalogs.

Wall-Mounted Shelves

Wall-mounted shelving can be simple, such as a bracket-supported single board that showcases one lovely object, or complex, such as an expanse ample enough to hold a library or

pantry. It can be decorative, featuring a piece of glass or marble resting on elegant antique brackets in a formal bath, or recede from view, painted to match the wall behind it. Depending upon how they are constructed, wall-mounted shelves can be open at the ends or encased, and can be at fixed or adjustable heights.

Coated wire shelves are one example of the ready-made and easy-to-install wall-mounted shelving that is widely available in home stores. The components available for these systems make them adaptable to many situations, but once installed this particular style is not adjustable. One of the quickest and easiest ways to set up an adjustable wall-mounted shelf system is to use surface-mounted standards, brackets, and plank shelves finished however you desire. There are a number of these systems readily available; each features compatible component parts in a variety of sizes, and all you usually need to install them is a screwdriver and some wall anchors. Hardware stores and lumber yards carry many styles of standards and brackets, and some also offer prefinished shelves or will cut stock lumber to your specifications for a nominal charge. The standard-and-bracket system offers numerous and flexible design possibilities because it is so easy to combine shelves of assorted depths and lengths in one area. The one **on the left of page 238** is set up as a home office, with a deep shelf as a desk top and shallower ones for books above. Because the top shelf spans only half the wall, there is room for taller items next to it on the shelf below. Many of these systems include useful accessories that clip onto the standards, such as the bookend seen in the middle of the shelf over the desk.

With somewhat more sophisticated carpentry skills, you can build and hang a shelf system like the one **on the right of page 238**. Here a carcass of open boxes was designed to accommodate a variety of books and papers and was fitted with a hinged shelf that folds down to become a work surface. **At lower left**, a similar system on a larger scale provides the framework for a display of crockery and gameboards. Because this collection is so beautifully assembled, it makes a strong graphic pattern against the wall, while the white shelving recedes into the same-color background.

© William B. Seitz

If you are installing wall-mounted shelving in an area where it could be an obstacle in your usual traffic pattern—adjacent to a doorway, for instance—you might consider rounding corners that protrude into the room. This will allow you to make the shelves as long and wide as possible. The plastic laminate–covered kitchen shelves **on the right of page 239** have a retro look that appeals to lovers of the 1950s. They are quite cheery filled with primary-color cookware and accessories, and they won't do too much damage to your shins should you turn past them too sharply.

Because the stone wall and long, narrow proportions make the galley kitchen **at left** feel dark and a bit cramped, open

shelves are a good storage choice; a wall of cupboard doors would make a small space like this one feel claustrophobic. Because these shelves have such a long span, they are cut from substantial planks to keep them from bowing in the middle. Their simple construction and natural finish are in keeping with the rustic atmosphere of this converted mill. Note the shallow shelves between the framing timbers on the rear wall.

The construction material and finish applied can give open shelves a practical, dressy, sophisticated, whimsical, or demure demeanor, and you will probably choose them to complement the rest of the decor in your room. Small display shelves might be worked metal or ornately carved wood, or have a faux finish; bathroom shelves might be glass or marble, which are elegant and resistant to steam damage; closet, kitchen, or workroom shelves might be wire, plastic laminate, or painted wood; and library shelves might be beautifully grained wood with a natural finish. Even if the shelves themselves are nondescript, you can give them a bit of character by applying a decorative edging. The old pantry shelves **at left** are faced with a narrow wallpaper border that perks them up; it also makes the assorted contents seem more visually cohesive. There are any number of edging options: you can use lace or ribbon instead of wallpaper, line the shelves with cloth or paper doilies that scallop over the edges, stencil or even woodburn a motif right onto the shelf itself, or simply paint the edge a contrasting color.

FREESTANDING STORAGE FURNITURE

Freestanding furniture can provide some of the most beautiful as well as most functional storage in a home. In older homes where closets are limited, storage furniture can be absolutely essential. In other homes there can be less need for it, but even where good storage is built into the home, our eyes appreciate the style, character, and focus that an elegant secretary, wonderful armoire, quaint country cupboard, or marble-topped bureau can add to a room.

Freestanding storage furniture can offer relatively large undivided interior space, like a blanket chest or trunk, or hanging storage, like an armoire, or it can be partitioned with shelves, drawers or cubbyholes in any number of configurations. Most pieces have accepted uses—linens, blankets, clothing, tableware, tools, correspondence—but there is no reason to limit them to the conventional if they will suit some other purpose and look attractive at the same time. You can put sweaters in a blanket chest, table linens or office supplies in a bureau, or tapes or records in the cupboards of a Welsh dresser; you can even use a pie safe as a liquor cabinet.

When planning to use freestanding storage furniture, decide whether its primary purpose is decorative or functional. If you must have a place to put your stereo system, it will not do you any good to buy an old country cupboard that is too small to hold the components—no matter how great it would look in the room. A blanket chest can make a terrific coffee table as long as you don't need constant access to the things stashed under the lid. Analyze the storage potential of a freestanding piece the same way you would a built-in one, making sure that the things you need to store will fit efficiently in the inner compartments. Most types of storage furniture are available in contemporary or period (antique and reproduction) styles in all degrees of formality, so you can choose each piece to complement the rest of your decor. And if you move, it can go with you, so you can consider it an investment.

If closet space is in short supply you might want to supplement it with a wardrobe or armoire. These pieces were standard in most pre–twentieth century homes, and antique or reproduction examples can be found in many styles and sizes. Armoires are almost always fitted with a hanging bar; many have interior shelves and drawers as well; and some also have exterior drawers. If you do not need hanging storage you can add

© William B. Seitz

shelves to the interior. If storage needs are not vast, in a guest room for instance, an armoire can take the place of both closet and bureau. The armoire on the back wall of the room **above** is a country piece with lovely proportions. Its flat top provides additional storage—if every centimeter of storage potential is important to you, stay away from models with curved tops. Also in this room is a marvelous secretary. Many of us have grown used to home offices where computers are used for correspondence, but an elegant desk or secretary is much nicer to look at in a living area and can showcase collectibles or a small library as well as store stationery supplies.

China cupboards, breakfronts, and sideboards can all provide storage for tableware and linens. Some have open shelves; some are enclosed with solid or glass-paned doors; some include drawers as well; some offer a broad open surface for serving or display; and many combine several of these options. Those

© Bruce McCandless

cooking gear as well as some decorative accessories. Mundane items like onions, canisters, and jams are charmingly displayed, while the pitcher of flowers and the cutwork napkins trimming the shelves add a pretty touch.

Some antique storage pieces are loved for their inherent charm, and even if contemporary lifestyles have really made them obsolete, they can make up for their lack of practicality with lots of character. Hoosier Beauties like the one **at left** were once thought marvelous as small and self-contained kitchen

with glass-paned doors or open shelves can be lovely settings in which to display tableware or collectibles. A large and rather rustic Welsh dresser like the one **on page 243** can double as a sideboard in a country dining room; because it is close to the kitchen, this one is used almost like a pantry, storing everyday workstations; they have built-in bins for flour, small shelves for cans and jars, drawers for utensils and linens, a larger cupboard for pots and pans, and a pull-out counter to work on. They don't hold enough of anything to be really useful unless you cook infrequently, but they can supplement other storage or show off collectibles, and they always make a room feel homey.

Pie safes—wooden cupboards with ventilated doors that let the air circulate but kept out the flies—were common before modern refrigeration superseded them. The doors were sometimes screened, or often, they had beautifully punched tin panels, as the one **at left** does. Today they are prized as folk furniture, and if they suit your decor, can be placed attractively almost anywhere and used to store anything from linens to books to kitchen goods; they are still fine for short-term pie storage as well.

There are many other kinds of freestanding storage furniture, from the common bedroom dresser to architects' flat files, so if you want to supplement your storage you should be able to find or adapt a piece to meet almost any need. Not all pieces are monumental or even particularly expensive; office file cabinets are a classic example of freestanding and readily available storage pieces, and taborets (which have swing-out drawers) like the one seen in the tiny drafting closet on page 213 are another. There are all sorts of other small cabinets made in a variety of materials. Wicker, which lends a touch of nostalgia, is often chosen for small cupboards in bathrooms, babies' rooms, or summer houses. The chest of drawers **at right** is made of molded plastic, which is modern and clinical and works well in studios and baths.

Be clear about your requirements and think creatively when you shop for freestanding storage furniture. If you are considering an antique or one-of-a-kind piece, take a Polaroid of it, note the measurements, and then think about it at home before you buy it. If you are buying a new piece, try to get the manufacturer's catalog, which will usually have clear photos and list all the specs, so that you can do the same.

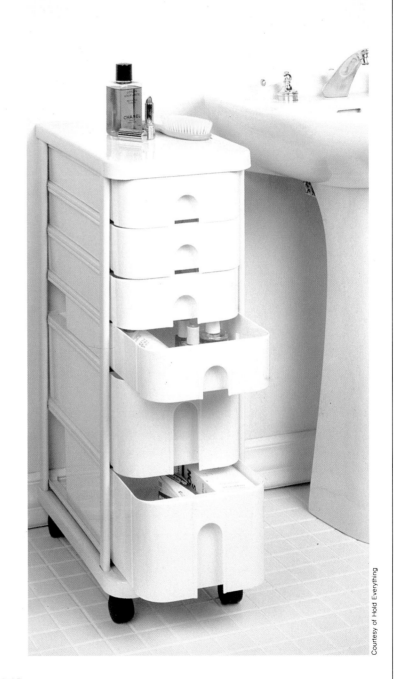

Taking Advantage of Odd Spaces

Many homes have oddly shaped, inaccessible, and unused spaces that can be adapted to provide valuable storage space. Sometimes this is just a matter of devising cleverly shaped shelves, and sometimes real head-scratching carpentry is involved, but if you can identify a potential storage space, there is a good chance you can put it to work.

Under the Stairs

If the stairs in your home do not rise in a well, there is a good chance that the space underneath them is just waiting to be claimed. While it is not uncommon to find a closet under the stairs, these are often approached through the narrow end, where there is ample headroom, and then rapidly taper down so that you end up crawling over things to reach the back. It is often more efficient to approach the space under the stairs from one side; you can cut in a series of cupboards or drawers, or remove the wall and install shelves under the steps. Consider using this space for something that would take up valuable floor space if it were elsewhere in the room. You can build a sound system into the space under the stairs, or a library, or if the area is big enough, turn it into a cozy reading alcove. In the home **at the top of page 247**, a small kitchen is tucked against the stairs, and careful planning has made good use of every centimeter of space. The L-shaped counter and cabinets are topped with a flight of shelves. A short cubby at the low end holds trash cans and a swivel bar for drying dish towels. The side of the staircase makes a nice backdrop for collectible plates and dried flowers.

Under the Eaves

Because it is impossible to stand upright under sloping eaves, the space beneath them is often underused. This is an ideal place to claim for storage. You can frame the equivalent of a built-in dresser under the eaves, with drawer fronts in any style you like. If there is a short interior wall—called a knee wall—running under the eaves, you can cut a door into it, giving access to the empty area under the sloping roof beyond. Although you will have to crawl into this space, it can provide a good home to infrequently used things such as suitcases, out-of-season clothing, or old papers; just be sure that anything you put there is properly packed if the space is unfinished. The doors set into the knee wall **at bottom left** open to reveal a swingout shelf unit, which provides handy recessed storage and takes advantage of what height there is; it also can be pivoted into the room to give access to the larger storage area beyond.

You can also build a sit-down workspace under the eaves. The knee wall of the two-person home office **at bottom right** has been fitted with a long bank of built-in lateral file cabinets topped by a desk-height counter. Small drawers and cubbyholes are tucked at the back. A small, bridgelike desk top links the files with the central desk, and you can slide your knees under this when using the computer. A rolling office chair allows sitting access to any of the cabinets and prevents banged heads.

© Jennifer Levy

© Jennifer Levy

© Bill Rothschild

STORAGE ACCESSORIES

Closets and storage areas are general spaces in which to put things; storage units are particular furnishings to fill with possessions. However, sometimes neither of these is divided finely enough to be completely practical. Most of the things we store for everyday use are small or awkwardly shaped —individual items of clothing, jewelry, cookware, tools, papers, office supplies—and tend to fall into a jumble unless our closets, cupboards, shelves, and drawers are fitted with accessory compartments to contain them neatly. And then there are all sorts of things that we need to store for occasional or seasonal use; we want these to be protected from dirt and pests in easy-to-handle containers even if we don't want everyday access to them. Additionally, many of us are making a concerted effort to recycle some or all of our trash, and this creates a need for complex sorting and storage systems, which must often be squeezed into an already tight kitchen, pantry, or garage space. Fortunately, many manufacturers have addressed all of these various space problems by making hundreds of storage accessories that are handy for imposing order on clutter.

Begin your quest for the perfect storage accessories with an analysis of the items to be stored and then determine whether you need container storage, such as boxes, bins, and bags, or wall-hanging storage, such as hooks, pegboards, and wall grids. Then decide how important the look of the accessories is to you; if function is more important than aesthetics, your options will be greater, but if aesthetics rule you should still have plenty to choose from.

Look in home stores and catalogs, and hardware and office supply stores, and don't be shy about asking for help, for many vendors can order storage accessories for you from their wholesale suppliers even if they don't stock the particular item you are looking for. Look in the phone book for commercial suppliers as well; wholesalers who supply institutions such as schools, hospitals, or restaurants will sometimes be willing to accommodate you. And don't overlook antique and second-hand shops, which often have wonderful old boxes and tins that could be just what you need—especially if you live in an old or reproduction house where plastic might seem out of place—as in the rustic country home **on page 248**, where the pantry shelves are filled with old barrels and tins, looking much as they might have a hundred years ago. (If this is a bit too rustic for you, consider sealing your staples in plastic bags before putting them into the bins.)

249

HANDY CONTAINERS

There are many conventional devices designed for specific storage purposes as well as all sorts of interesting and perhaps unexpected containers that might be adapted to your needs, so be flexible and creative as you search for storage accessories. Things designed for one purpose might be just as suitable for another: stacking letter trays meant for the desk top can hold tea towels and napkins in a linen closet; small-parts cabinets can hold jewelry or sewing notions as well as nuts and bolts; old thread cabinets are great for art supplies. And think of things you can recycle into storage containers yourself: large spackle buckets are great for birdseed or potting soil; olive oil tins with the tops removed can hold all sorts of utensils; and assorted screw-top jars can store spices and grains purchased in bulk (if you paint the lids all one color, they'll look organized).

Storage Bins and Drawers

You can find storage bins in plastic, wire, wood, cardboard, metal, and even glass and ceramic, and choose further from airtight or ventilated styles in sizes that hold just about anything. From the most common kitchen canister to the most sophisticated toolbox, from a pretty chintz-covered bandbox to a practical and all-purpose plastic bin with snap-on lid, from the utilitarian small-parts cabinet to the luxury of under-bed cedar drawers, there is a ready-made bin just waiting to store anything you'd like to put away—with verve and style if you wish.

Whether you are looking for heavy-duty bins for the basement and garage, dampness- and pest-proof canisters for the pantry, or in-closet storage to take the place of a dresser, you'll find options in design and aesthetics as well as material and size. Hundreds of handy containers with practical and sometimes very sophisticated styling, in a world of color and surface pattern, are out there, waiting to be stacked, lined up on shelves, and slid or rolled under bed, workbench, or desk.

Your choice of storage bins will be guided by the size, weight, and perishability of what you want to put in them, as well as where you want to put them, whether in an enclosed or open space, or on the floor or a shelf. Other considerations will be whether you need everyday access to them, and whether or not you want to be able to see the contents. Think about filling storage bins the same way you would drawers: put large items in large bins, small items in small ones, and fold or arrange things so as to use the interior space efficiently.

For utility storage, choose sturdy bins with secure lids such as those **below**. These stand up well when exposed to the elements and have handles for easy moving and recessed lids for secure stacking; they are lightweight for their strength and can

Courtesy of Rubber Maid Inc.

be nested when empty. Bins such as these make ideal storage not only for tools but for such items as out-of-season clothing or blankets, and birdseed or dried pet food. Because they are easy to move and fairly watertight, they are great for camping gear or on-the-go work equipment. If you need to secure them from pests such as raccoons, clip stretchable shock cords from handle to handle over the tops. Note the utility rack in the rear of this photo; a variety of sliding hooks and clips makes it easy to customize.

Translucent plastic bins such as those **above** come in a variety of small sizes, and a quick glance is all that is needed to reveal their contents. They are great for clothing, shoes, and accessories; craft, art, and office supplies; stationery; and games and toys with many parts. They can sit individually on shelves or in stacks, but be wary of stacking them too high as access will be inconvenient. Closet accessory shops and catalogs sometimes carry plastic drawers in similar sizes. If plastic is not to your taste, there are a variety of paper- and cloth-covered boxes and drawers intended for office and closet use; these may be sturdy or fragile, depending on their construction, and they are sometimes very attractive.

Open stacking bins provide easy access to all types of gear. Falling somewhere between shelves and drawers, they are deep enough to hold assorted, oddly shaped items securely. They are lightweight but steady on their feet and can be used in closets or out in the open, as you wish; arrange several stacks together against a wall and you have a quick, self-supporting

storage system for workshop or playroom. Those **on the right of page 251** come in a variety of bright colors that just might encourage children to keep their stuff picked up. Some models, such as those **at lower left**, can be stacked onto casters, making them ideal for under-counter storage.

In a similar vein, there are wire baskets that slide like drawers into stationary or rolling frames. Aesthetically, these have a light, refined look that makes them suitable for office, bath, or kitchen use (laminate or butcher block tops are available for some models), as well as for installation in laundry, workshop, and of course, closet. Wire bins are also available in under-shelf styles like the one **at right**. These slide onto any shelf and are extremely versatile; they can be used as letter trays or temporary files on bookshelves over a desk; added to a linen closet for tea towels, face cloths, or soaps; or placed in a clothes closet for lingerie.

It would be a shame to overlook traditional baskets—wood, straw, grass, reed, and vine—in any discussion of storage bins. Because baskets are decorative and not usually designed to stack or even to sit squarely on a shelf, they are perhaps best used when your storage system is open to view. They come in all shapes, sizes, and colors and can be remarkably inexpensive or astonishingly costly. Some have lids; some have handles and can be hung from hooks in the ceiling; and some stack neatly. Large, sturdy baskets make great laundry hampers or toy chests, while smaller ones can hold magazines, needlework projects, gardening tools, or whatever you like.

Organizing Drawers and Cupboards
Your cupboards and drawers, whether in built-in or freestanding furniture, may have adequate but inefficient storage space. A walk down the aisles of any office-supply, hardware, or houseware store should offer you all sorts of add-on storage-enhancing accessories. These are usually made of metal, molded plastic, or coated wire and are designed to fit into drawers, sit on cabinet shelves, or be mounted inside cupboard doors. For media

Courtesy of Heller Inc.

Courtesy of Heller Inc.

and computer needs, there are racks for audio and video tapes, CDs, and floppy disks. For the office there are paper sorters, in-drawer and shelf filing systems, and divided trays for small supplies. For the kitchen, there are lazy Susans and pantry racks for staples; small utility bins with handles for cleaning aids; racks and bins for pots, pans, and lids; spice racks for shelf, door, or drawer; and divided bins for flatware—some incorporating an upper sliding tray for extra storage—and more.

An assortment of handy kitchen cupboard organizing devices is shown **at the top of page 254**, just a few of the many styles that are available. Note the dispenser caddies for boxes of plastic bags, which allow one-handed extraction, and the iron rack, which will store both iron and board on the inside of a door. Some small storage accessories can be adjusted to fit a particular space; others can be configured to suit your needs. **On the bottom of page 254** are two that come predivided, and they will go a long way to helping you get organized. When looking for cupboard organizers, remember that every discipline has its own paraphernalia and so you should investigate vendors who specialize in yours first, then check out others since one person's handy desk organizer might be another's needlework center.

Courtesy of Rubber Maid Inc.

Clothing Storage Accessories While many multi-purpose bins and drawers are perfectly suitable for clothing storage, there is a whole world of accessories designed specifically to protect shoes and hanging and folded garments. These are generally soft, constructed of quilted fabric or canvas, and sometimes divided into compartments and partially reinforced with cardboard. Soft closet accessories are often very attractive and usually rather costly. Those that zip closed offer good, dust-free storage and can be used with aromatic pomanders and sachets or moth repellent (follow the manufacturer's instructions) for off-season storage. The line of accessories in the photo **at right** includes a shoe bag, a hanging garment bag, a sweater bag, and a sweater or blanket box.

There are also wood, metal, and plastic racks designed to store ties, belts, scarves, and shoes; some examples of these can be seen in chapter one.

Courtesy of Hold Everything

Trash and Recycling Systems

It seems as though everything we buy today comes in a protective box or wrapper that is discarded as soon as we get it home. Manufacturers everywhere are trying to cut down on unnecessary packaging, and minimal wrappings are beginning to appear, but boxes and bags are unlikely to ever disappear completely, and cans and bottles will be essential for food packaging for years to come. Many communities have voluntary or mandatory recycling programs, and consumers are ever more eager to participate. Doing so means sorting household trash into several categories and storing items that will be picked up

Courtesy of Heller Inc.

as well as those that will be brought to a drop-off center. Even if you have a large basement or garage so that space is not a problem, you need an organized system of containers that are easy to transport, empty, and clean.

Each community recycles different materials, and each household's needs are different, but there are quite a few con-

tainers available to meet them all. While many of these are available in local stores, some of the newer ones are easier to find in mail-order catalogs, so keep your eyes open.

If you compost your vegetable scraps, you can use a small and inexpensive triangular bin that sits inside one corner of your sink—these are available in most houseware stores—or invest